YEAR
ONE
OF
THE
EMPIRE

YEAR ONE OF THE EMPIRE

A PLAY OF AMERICAN POLITICS, WAR, AND PROTEST
TAKEN FROM THE HISTORICAL RECORD

ELINOR FUCHS

AND

JOYCE ANTLER

HOUGHTON MIFFLIN COMPANY BOSTON

1973

FIRST PRINTING   C

PRINTED IN THE UNITED STATES OF AMERICA

CAUTION: *Year One of the Empire*
is the sole property of the copyright owners
and is fully protected by copyright.
It may not be acted by professionals
or amateurs without written permission
and the payment of a royalty.
All rights, including professional, amateur, stock, radio
broadcasting, television, motion picture, recitation, lecturing,
public reading, and the rights of translation
into foreign languages are reserved.
All inquiries should be addressed
to the Authors' agent, Lois Berman,
530 East 72nd Street,
New York, N.Y. 10021.

Library of Congress Cataloging in Publication Data
Fuchs, Elinor.
   Year one of the empire.
   Bibliography: p.
   1. Philippine Islands—History—Insurrection, 1899–
1901—Drama.   I. Antler, Joyce, joint author.
II. Title.
PS3556.U3Y4   812'.5'4   72–6812
ISBN 0-395-15565-7   ISBN 0-395-18094-5 (pbk.)

. . . This Philippine year has been one of illusion succeeding illusion, and hope deferred. The war has dragged on its misery beyond all computation . . . We have disabled ourselves from expressing sympathy with any oppressed people on earth. Our generous professions of love for liberty stick in our throats . . . as we think of what we have been doing in this Year One of our new Empire.

If the events of the past twelvemonth have been thus melancholy for ourselves . . . what would a . . . Filipino say had been the chief import of the year past to his people? He would have a terrible array of disasters to specify . . . Liberty crushed to earth by the land of liberty . . . broken promises . . . trenches full of Filipino dead . . . smoking heaps where once were happy villages . . . desolate fields . . . ruined industries . . . starving women and children . . .

an editorial in *The Nation*,
February 8, 1900

ACKNOWLEDGMENTS

We gratefully acknowledge the permission of the Massachusetts Historical Society to adapt portions of the Lodge-Roosevelt correspondence, and thank the Library of Congress for the use of manuscript collections of several of the leading characters.

We wish to express our warm thanks to a number of people who generously offered us their time and knowledge. Albert C. Bermel and Daniel Gerould of the theatre departments of Lehman College and the City University of New York, and historians David Trask, Bernard Semmel, Daniel Fox, and Robert Marcus of the State University of New York at Stony Brook encouraged our attempt to join history and theatre. We are indebted to historian Daniel B. Schirmer, who gave us many valuable suggestions. Astute criticisms of our early drafts were offered by Stephen Aaron of the drama faculty of The Juilliard School, Tom and Joyce Cole, Patricia Cumming of M.I.T., Judith Pearlman, Sophy Burnham, and director Harold Stone, Jr. We owe special thanks to our agent, Lois Berman, for her skill and judgment in our behalf.

Finally, our husbands, Michael Oakes Finkelstein and Stephen Antler, read and reread our work. For their many contributions we are deeply grateful.

CONTENTS

AUTHORS' PREFACE

This is a play about America's first land war in Asia, taken from hundreds of documentary sources. We view this forgotten turn-of-the-century conflict as an American watershed. It was the moment when America ceased to be the "son of the morning" (so the disillusioned William Dean Howells put it) and took up a career as an imperial power.

Few Americans know that the United States fought a three-year guerrilla war in the Philippine Islands from 1899 to 1902. That war, and the national protest movement against it, have been the best-kept secrets in American history. By contrast, everyone knows about the little war with Spain which directly preceded our Philippine involvement. It has survived in its nostalgic revision as a charming, if excessive, display of adolescent vigor.

The Philippine War lends itself to no such scenic designer's view of history. The war was the most savage the U.S. had ever fought. By the end, the American army's practices of torture, reconcentration, and the massacre of Filipino civilians had created a national uproar, resulting in the court-martials of a general and several lesser officers.

The conquest of the Philippines marked a radical departure from American tradition. Expansion was forcefully extended for the first time to colonies outside the Western Hemisphere. For the first time, American policy was advanced by the suppression of nationalist aspirations abroad. A century of commitment to the cause of democratic revolution was reversed.

The United States went to war in 1898 in support of such a revolution in Cuba. It was a war for "humanity" and "Cuba libre." When the U.S. Navy, in the opening move of the war, destroyed the Spanish fleet at Manila, native leaders assumed that America's self-proclaimed ideals extended also to the Philippines, where a revolution against Spanish rule had barely ended. Now they assembled an army to help America oust Spain from the islands, declared national independence, and set up a constitutional government, the first republic in Asia.

After the war, Cuba got her freedom (later qualified by the Platt Amendment), but America kept the rest of the Spanish empire: Guam, Puerto Rico, and the "pearl of the Orient," the Philippines. As President McKinley explained to the French ambassador (with the "curious logic" derided by an opposition senator), "the American people would not accept it if we did not obtain some advantage . . . from the sacrifices" the U.S. made in setting the islands free. A few months later the Filipino army, barefoot, ill-armed, untrained, was fighting for independence against the impressive American military force stationed in the islands.

To Americans today, now sophisticates in guerrilla warfare, the stumbling course of our first attempt at counter-insurgency will seem familiar. Official assurances that the war was over, followed by calls for reinforcements. Towns taken one month, retaken the next. Villages officially loyal to the U.S. simultaneously administered by *insurrectos*. The failure of search-and-destroy tactics; the failure of pacification efforts.

Filipinos were "niggers" to the American soldiers and "Apaches" to Vice-President Roosevelt. Beyond this casual arrogance, the broader racial implications of the war were seized on in both countries. A prominent Philippine leader justified resistance to American rule on racial grounds. His people would never have justice, he said, under "a nation that hates the colored race with a mortal hatred." Former abolitionists in America pointed out that while the government made war against a people of color abroad, Negroes in the South were suffering mob violence and systematic disfranchisement. A black American bishop who was president of the Afro-American Congress, the leading black organization in America, charged that "had the Filipinos been white . . . the war would have been ended and their independence granted long ago."

In spite of superior forces and sophisticated weaponry, the American military command could not bring about the easy victory it anticipated. At least four thousand American soldiers died in the war and thousands more were wounded. At the height of the fighting, some seventy thousand American troops were engaged. Altogether about one hundred twenty-eight thousand Americans served in the islands. It is hard to believe that a war of this magnitude has been so thoroughly forgotten.

For the Philippines, the war was a holocaust. A Republican congressman who toured the islands in 1902 returned home with what he called "the secret of pacification": "Our soldiers took no prisoners, they kept no records; they simply swept the country, and wherever and whenever they could get hold of a Filipino, they killed him." Hundreds of thousands of Filipinos died through war and related causes. Countless towns and villages were destroyed. The agriculture of the islands was utterly ruined. Starvation was widespread for years after the end of the war.

For America, the new venture into empire produced a moral crisis exceeded only by the crisis over slavery. The national debate on the question of the Philippines was waged in Congress, churches, farm and labor forums, universities, state legislatures, and in every journal of opinion in the country. It was no mere discussion of foreign policy alternatives, but a search, and seen as such by advocates on either side, into the meaning of the American experience. The outcome would determine the "twentieth-century contribution of the American nation to the world."

The protest against imperialism drew hundreds of thousands

of supporters. An Anti-Imperialist League was founded in Boston in 1898. Within a year there were over one hundred active anti-imperialist leagues across the country, and a national center in Chicago. The anti-imperialists were a virtual Who's Who of their time. They included former Presidents Grover Cleveland and Benjamin Harrison; university presidents like Charles Eliot of Harvard and David Starr Jordan of Leland Stanford; industrialists, labor leaders, and reformers, such as Andrew Carnegie, Samuel Gompers, Clarence Darrow, Carl Schurz, Jane Addams; and many leading writers and intellectuals — among them Mark Twain, William Dean Howells, Edgar Lee Masters, William Vaughn Moody, William James, John Dewey, and Thorstein Veblen.

"Imperialism" was a major issue of the 1900 election. "The President's war" could be stopped only by getting rid of the President, the opposition argued. McKinley's encroachment on the authority of Congress (which had never declared war on the Philippines) troubled anti-imperialists. According to Champ Clark of Missouri, the President had turned Congress into "an animated cash register" for the payment of war expenses. Polemicist Morrison Swift proposed radical remedies. "Not only should the President be impeached . . . but action for murder in the first degree should be brought against him," he raged. "Discrimination is what I protest." Why "hang small murderers," and elect "vast ones to a second term"?

On the other side were the expansionists: Theodore Roosevelt, Henry Cabot Lodge, Albert Beveridge, and others who saw American world leadership glimmering just beyond this necessary extension of U.S. territory, trade, and global influence. They condemned the anti-imperialists (the "aunties") as cowards and traitors, and charged that the "opposition to the war was the chief factor in prolonging it."

The anti-imperialist leaders were not young radicals. Many of them had awakened into politics fifty years earlier in the abolitionist crusade. Now again they believed that American founding principles were betrayed by the denial of human freedom. But the drift of the times was against them. Young progressives thought their concern with individual human liberties was old-fashioned, and their view of America as a moral entity narrow and inflexible. The America of the anti-imperialist was chaste, principled, and unaggrandizing; Roosevelt's America was young, virile, exuberant, and expanding. This basic clash of attitudes about the ideal nature of the American nation underlay the struggle over imperialism.

The anti-imperialists never recovered their faith in the future of America, which they saw threatened by the growth of empire and military power. The country had "thrown away its ancient principles" and "joined the common pack of wolves," said William James in sorrow and disgust. America would probably be richer and stronger, grieved Howells, but "freedom . . . will never again shriek when Kosciusko falls." Roosevelt impatiently dismissed the minor "obstruction and clamor" of these short-sighted "prophets of disaster." Yet today, the message of the anti-imperialists seems inescapably prophetic, not only because we have passed through a similarly disillusioning war, but because there may in fact be no appeal from their judgment on the limits of the American possibility.

We have been asked why we wrote a play and not an historical narrative. The question assumes vaguely either that a play is an unsuitable vehicle for history, or that history, at least as we have used it, without romantic invention, is uncongenial to the theatre.

Our aim would not have been served by such a narrative. We were more interested in texture than interpretation. We were more interested in transmitting a direct experience of people and events than in explaining why history turned out as it did. We wanted to transpose history to the present tense, and restore a sense of the compromises, accidents, and human blunders that go to make up an immutable record. We wanted to mask the historian's voice, which would have been a barrier between our audience and the fresh experience of our material. This accessibility the dramatic form encourages.

Then, too, this is no history of merely antiquarian interest. In this story is the link between the recent horrific America of Vietnam, and the America "of the quiet chamber of the fathers in Philadelphia," as one of our characters, Senator George Hoar, says. It is a necessary story in American cosmogony. To us, it demanded the public witnessing of theatre.

Public witnessings are rare enough in American theatre, where only diversion or "pure" art (and little of that) are sought. Our theatre has virtually no role for public discussion, or for any other manner of exploring our nearest concerns as an American people. Our theatre does not treat us as a people, in fact, but as a random collection of individuals. In the deepest sense, ours is a theatre of private enterprise. Its economic base and its prevailing subject have a common identity.

We hear that the problem is the audience — there is no audience for theatre in the United States. But perhaps there is a latent audience in America for a theatre that hardly exists: a truly public kind of theatre that is serious, broadly accessible, and directed in one way or another to our shared, most urgent interests. Such a theatre could serve to put us in touch with ourselves as a people. It could use for its material all elements of American commonality, among them the intermittent episodes of almost mythic power in American history. We made this play with such a theatre in mind.

1973   Elinor Fuchs
                                                       Joyce Antler

YEAR
ONE
OF
THE
EMPIRE

CAST OF CHARACTERS

IN THE WHITE HOUSE

William McKinley
Theodore Roosevelt
formerly: *New York City Police Commissioner, Assistant Secretary of the Navy, Colonel of the First United States Volunteer Cavalry, Governor of New York State, and candidate for Vice-President of the United States*

IN THE UNITED STATES SENATE

Republicans
Albert J. Beveridge, Indiana
Joseph Foraker, Ohio
George Frisbie Hoar, Massachusetts
Henry Cabot Lodge, Massachusetts
William Mason, Illinois
Richard Pettigrew, South Dakota
Redfield Proctor, Vermont
John Spooner, Wisconsin

Democrats
William Allen, Nebraska (Democrat-Populist)
Augustus Bacon, Georgia
Edward Carmack, Tennessee
Benjamin ("Pitchfork Ben") Tillman, South Carolina

CABINET MEMBERS

Secretary of State John Hay
Secretary of the Navy John Davis Long
Secretary of War Elihu Root

ANTI-IMPERIALISTS

Edward Atkinson
George Boutwell
Andrew Carnegie
The Reverend Joseph Mendl
Herbert Myrick
Carl Schurz
Moorfield Storey
Mark Twain

PARTY BOSSES

Richard Croker, Tammany Leader, New York City
Senator Marcus Alonzo Hanna, Republican, Ohio
Senator Thomas Collier Platt, Republican, New York
Senator Matthew Quay, Republican, Pennsylvania

A FRIEND OF THE ADMINISTRATION

H. H. Kohlsaat

AN OFFICER OF THE U.S. NAVY

Commodore George Dewey

OFFICERS OF THE U.S. ARMY

Brigadier General James Franklin Bell
Major General Adna R. Chaffee
First Lieutenant Grover Flint
Brigadier General Frederick Funston
Major Cornelius Gardener
Brigadier General Robert P. Hughes
Major General Arthur MacArthur

Major General Elwell S. Otis
Major General William Shafter
Brigadier General Jacob ("Hell-Roaring Jake") Smith
Colonel Arthur Wagner
Major General Joseph Wheeler

U.S. ARMY VOLUNTEERS

Dudley Dean
Private A. F. Miller
Corporal Richard T. O'Brien
Private William Lewis Smith

IN HAVANA

Señor Don Tomas Pidal

IN MANILA

Señorita Juliana Lopez

OBSERVERS

Henry Adams
Mr. Dooley and Mr. Hennessey

AND

Aides, Clerks, Correspondents, Photographers, Reporters, Senators, Soldiers, Spokesmen, Others

ACT ONE

America, before McKinley

HENRY ADAMS *stands alone on a darkened stage.*

ADAMS
America, drifting in the dead water of the end of the century, and during this last decade everyone talked and seemed to feel end-of-century.

If there was such a thing in America as an earnest impulse, an energy or a thought outside of dollars and cents, one could not find it. No period so thoroughly ordinary had been known in American politics since Christopher Columbus first disturbed the balance of American society.

Everywhere was slack water. What was worse, the redeeming *energy* of Americans, which had generally served as the resource of minds otherwise vacant, showed signs of check. One met a sort of stagnation, a creeping paralysis. Decline was everywhere.

Yet one could feel that something new and curious was about to happen to the world. The new American had turned his back on the nineteenth century before he was done with it.

Parade music drifts onto the stage.

So it was, in November of 1896, that one went home, with everyone else, to elect William McKinley President of the United States, and to start the world anew.

A jubilant CROWD *comes on with a parade float bearing a smiling likeness of* WILLIAM McKINLEY. *They carry campaign signs — "Prosperity," "Sanity," "Gold," "America," "Down with Bryan," "Sound Money," "The Grand Old Party," "McKinley Will Bring Us Back." They follow the float off.* ADAMS *has disappeared in the crowd.*

2

Lunch at the McKinleys', Canton, Ohio

At one side, HENRY CABOT LODGE, *U.S. senator from Massachusetts: at forty-six, he is elegant and scholarly, "Boston incarnate," according to Adams — "English literature, English traditions, English taste." At the same time he is a politician with an instinct for the jugular.*

He is dictating a letter in a mood of considerable political satisfaction.

LODGE
The Honorable Theodore Roosevelt, Police Commissioner, New York City. Private. My dear Theodore.

I went to Canton, Ohio, Sunday night, and lunched Monday with President-elect McKinley.

Lights now rise on President-elect WILLIAM MCKINLEY, *solid and benign, at lunch.*

He asked me about Cuba, and I found he had given it a great deal of thought . . .

LODGE, *joins* MCKINLEY *at table, talking earnestly*
President Cleveland and the Democrats have not shown the slightest sympathy with the struggling Cubans. We cannot leave them under Spain. We have a duty there.

MCKINLEY, *sympathetic, but wary*
Naturally, Senator Lodge, I don't want to be obliged to go to war as soon as I come in.

LODGE
Naturally not.

MCKINLEY
My first ambition is to restore business and bring back good times.

LODGE, *reassuringly*
Oh, business wouldn't suffer from a fight with Spain. On the contrary, it would improve. But the issue is beyond business considerations.

MCKINLEY, *courteously*
I assure you I appreciate the momentous character of the Cuban question. We will need the strongest possible man in the State Department.

LODGE, *seizing the moment*
And you will need strong men in the military departments. You may be familiar with the work of my young friend Roosevelt.

MCKINLEY

Oh yes, I have great regard for him, great regard. I would like to have him in Washington, but where?

LODGE

Perhaps at Navy?

MCKINLEY

Navy. Yes, the Navy Department is possible. But I hope he has no (*seeking polite words*) preconceived plans to drive through the moment he gets in . . .

3

The New York City Police Department

Commissioner THEODORE ROOSEVELT *is reading the New York Evening Post in a spirit bordering on apoplexy. TR is in his mid-thirties, a man of extraordinary charm, self-confidence, and vigor. We may call him belligerent, but he raises belligerence to a new plane of consciousness. He is the idealist of the warring spirit, the apostle of manly virtue among the mammonites.*

TR, *throwing down the paper*
The clamor of the peace faction convinces me that this country needs a war!

dictating
Henry Cabot Lodge, U.S. Senate, Washington. Private.
The *Post* today is full of cowardly chatter for "peace at any price." (*striding about*) If we ever come to nothing as a nation it will be because of the "peace at any price" men —

with a certain flair for mimicry
— President Eliot of Harvard — that prattling foreigner, Carl Schurz — the futile sentimentalists of the international arbitration type . . . And the New York *Evening Post*, of course, which is ferociously attacking me as a "jingo."

Personally, I hope the fight will come soon. I don't care whether our seacoast cities are bombarded. The real danger is that we shall lose the great fighting features of our race, lose our moral spring, and become genuinely effete!

LODGE *is now at his desk on the other side of the stage.* TR *crosses to him genially.*

Of course I don't have a preconceived policy of any kind I want to push through . . .

LODGE
I told McKinley not to have the slightest uneasiness about it. I said I knew your views about the navy — they were just to push forward the policies of the last two or three administrations.

TR
That's it. Oh, Cabot, I think you are the staunchest, most loyal friend in the world!

5

4
Havana

Headlines shriek of Spanish atrocities in Cuba. At the same time, WAR CORRESPONDENTS *deliver newspaper reports.*

M A S S A C R E !

SLAUGHTER OF INNOCENT NONCOMBATANTS CONTINUES IN CUBA

SPAIN IS WAGING CAMPAIGN OF ATROCITIES

UNTRIED PRISONERS SHOT IN SQUADS

BODIES THROWN INTO TRENCHES AND LEFT UNBURIED

HORRIBLE CONDITIONS IN RECONCENTRATION CAMPS

AMERICAN TRAVELERS REPORT WIDESPREAD STARVATION AND DISEASE

SPANISH BARBARITIES SWELL INSURGENT RANKS BY THOUSANDS

FIRST CORRESPONDENT
Havana. Of the six Cuban provinces, two are now in the hands of the insurgents, and are called "Cuba Libre." In the four others, it is practically the entire Cuban population on the one side and the Spanish army on the other.

SECOND CORRESPONDENT
The Spanish government is driving hundreds of thousands of peasants from the countryside to fortified towns and villages called reconcentration camps. These are surrounded by trenches and barbed wire, and are closely guarded by armed

6

soldiers to keep the insurgents out and the *reconcentrados* in. Anyone found outside the enclosures is considered a rebel.

THIRD CORRESPONDENT
Horrible tales of butchery are being brought back from the interior by responsible men. Prisoners are being slaughtered in the fields, their bodies mutilated. Nothing but the intervention of some powerful nation can stop these scenes of bloodshed and destruction.

CORRESPONDENTS *gather about Senator* REDFIELD PROCTOR, *a fine New England gentleman of normally restrained judgment.*

PROCTOR
It is not war; it is desolation. It is the worst misery of which I ever had knowledge. I saw little children walking about with arms and chest terribly emaciated, eyes swollen, and abdomen bloated to three times the natural size. The physicians say they cannot be saved.

These — these reconcentration camps, so called, are virtual prison yards. The commonest sanitary provisions are impossible. I thought the press had overdrawn the picture, but my inquiries have been entirely outside sensational sources and — why — two hundred thousand noncombatants have died of starvation and disease . . .

his eyes filling
If our American people could see even a small fraction of the need, they would pour more freely from their liberal stores than ever before for any cause —

FIRST CORRESPONDENT
Senator Proctor, sir, will you propose action by the Administration in Washington?

7

PROCTOR, *fervently*
Something should be done . . .

SECOND CORRESPONDENT
Do you personally favor recognition of Cuban independence?

THIRD CORRESPONDENT
Do you favor armed American intervention, sir?

PROCTOR, *fending them off*
That is all, gentlemen, that is all.

5

Offices of Senator Lodge and Theodore Roosevelt

They are talking on the telephone, feet on desks.

LODGE
Theodore?

TR, *excitedly*
Cabot! Yes?

LODGE
I have just come from talking over the telephone with Senator Platt of New York, the venerable "Boss." I told him I was going to ask a favor of him, and then said what I wanted for you. He said he didn't feel ready to say he would support you, if you intended to go into the Navy Department and make war on him — or, as he put it, on the New York Republican "organization." (*all this with mild Brahmin amusement*)

8

I replied with some surprise that I didn't see how you came in contact with the "organization" in the Navy Department at all. He said — (*mimics Platt's cigar-in-teeth to the extent a Boston gentleman may do such things*) — "Oh yes, there is the Brooklyn Navy Yard."

They laugh.

TR, *howling*
The Navy Yard!!!

LODGE
Whether there is any real resistance to you in Washington I cannot tell, and the only, absolutely the only thing I can hear adverse is that there is a fear you will want to fight somebody at once.

TR, *wounded innocence*
I think that President McKinley would find that I wouldn't be in any way an (*searching for the word*) an agitator.

Besides, a war with Spain wouldn't be serious enough to cause much strain on the country. It would give our people something to think about that isn't material gain. It would benefit the military by trying them out in actual practice. (*daydreaming*) And it would be a splendid thing for the navy!

Lights rise on "Boss" PLATT of New York, chewing a cigar.

PLATT
I don't particularly like Theodore. He has been a disturbing element. But he can probably do less harm to the organization as Assistant Secretary of the Navy than anywhere else you can name. (*with a wave of the hand*) Let him have the job.

9

6

Cuba Libre

A ragged but dignified CUBAN PEASANT *sits center.*

THE SORROWS OF DON TOMAS PIDAL
A Reconcentrado

CUBAN, *addressing the audience*

I always lived in Punta Brava, and I was always happy until the war came. Our people there did not want war with the Spanish Government.

Then some of the valiant men from my country took their guns and said they would not leave a Spaniard alive on the island.

But, señores, I am not brave. I never talked loud in the *fonda*. I had a wife and five children. I had a good house, ten cows of fine milk, ten pigs on my land, two yokes of heavy work oxen. I had a field of pineapples and many strong mango trees. We ate twice a day. We could have eaten all day if we had so desired.

One day, a column of the Spanish soldiers came marching by my house and the officer said we must all go to town so there would be no one left to help the rebels hiding in the countryside. They burned my house and drove my beasts away. I could not get my money from the burning house. Then in my field the Spanish soldiers cut my boy to pieces, señores, cut him with the machetes until he was all over with blood. I went to the commandante to see what should be done, but he knew nothing about it.

They made me move inside a wire fence. They gave us no food. My two young children soon died, and about me many of my friends were dying like dogs. The oxcart came in the afternoon and they threw my two children into it like carrion. In that cart, señores, were twenty-two dead people. If I had five dollars, I could have gotten a box, but I did not have it. So my two little ones went to Guatoco on an oxcart loaded with dead like garbage — which is what the Spanish commandante said we were. My wife never dried her tears after that.

The days became harder. My people lay on the floor of our thatch hut and they had not the strength to warm water in the kettle. My other child died, and again the oxcart came. My oldest boy said he was going away and would not return. He got through the wire fence in the dark of night. I have not seen him since. I no longer look for him.

My wife grew weaker. I had hopes that by going through the fence every few nights I could keep her alive. One night I stole some food in the soldiers' kettle near a mess fire, and the men of the battalion fired many shots at me. Once a Cuban soldier fighting for Spain gave me a piece of fresh beef which I fed to my wife. I thought to save her with the beef, but she died that night in agony.

Then I ran away through the wire fence. I could not see my wife thrown on the dead wagon. I did not care if I was killed. I do not see, señores, why people who do not want war should have it. Señores, why have not the blue soldiers of your language come to us before we died?

7
The Senate Cloakroom

FIRST SENATOR
My God, isn't McKinley going to *do* anything?

SECOND SENATOR
I heard today he's sending a warship to Havana.

FIRST SENATOR
A ship? What in God's name will that do?

SECOND SENATOR
Well, the idea is to make a friendly visit but at the same time to make a show of strength —

FIRST SENATOR
That's ridiculous! It won't do a damn bit of *real* good, and it's like waving a match in an oil well.

A flash of light followed by a tremendous explosion — smaller explosions, sirens, bells, the screams of injured men. Headlines.

FEBRUARY 15, 1898

C R I S I S   A T   H A N D !

UNITED STATES BATTLESHIP MAINE BLOWN UP IN HAVANA HARBOR

AT LEAST 250 KILLED AND WOUNDED

CABINET IN SESSION

GROWING BELIEF IN SPANISH TREACHERY

**PRESIDENT McKINLEY BELIEVES EXPLOSION
WAS RESULT OF AN ACCIDENT**

**He Urges Public to Suspend Opinion
Until Further Report**

**Appoints Naval Court of Inquiry
to Investigate Disaster**

8

Office of the Secretary of the Navy

The Secretary, JOHN DAVIS LONG, *is scanning the newspapers. Dateline appears.*

FEBRUARY 25, 1898

LONG, *anxiously*
Public sentiment is very intense. The slightest spark is liable to
result in war with Spain.

Our great battleships are experiments which have never yet
been tried. And the horrors and costs and miseries of war itself are incalculable . . .

I had a terrible night, sleepless and nervous —

TR *enters with a buoyant stride, followed by a naval* AIDE.

TR
Mr. Secretary, you sent for me, sir?

LONG
Ah, Roosevelt.

13

TR, *exuberantly*
Did you see the newspapers, Mr. Secretary?

LONG
Roosevelt, I have decided to take the afternoon at home. I require sleep. You will be Acting Secretary. If you feel it essential to see someone, speak to the President, please.

TR, *walking him to the door*
Have a restful afternoon, Mr. Secretary. I'll take care of things.

LONG, *exhausted*
Thanks, Roosevelt.

TR, *to audience*
That may be the only Secretary of the United States Navy who was ever a member of the Massachusetts Peace Society.

briskly to AIDE
Now. There is work to be done.

AIDE, *whipping out a notebook*
Yessir!

TR
Acting Secretary of the Navy orders shipment, twenty cases of ten-inch projectiles from New York to Fort Monroe.

AIDE
Yessir!

TR
Orders carloads of twelve-inch projectiles from Albany to Fort Hamilton.

14

AIDE
Yessir!

TR
Requests immediate authority of Congress for fifteen hundred additional seamen.

AIDE
Yessir!

TR
And three hundred thousand tons of coal to Key West — use, possible invasion, Cuba.

AIDE
Yessir!

TR
Good. Take a cable.

A portentous pause: ROOSEVELT *is about to commit the most daring act of his career.*

Commodore George Dewey, Hong Kong. Secret. Keep full of coal. In the event of declaration war Spain, see that Spanish squadron does not leave Asiatic coast. Then, offensive operations in Philippine Islands. Roosevelt.

Lights rise on Commodore DEWEY, *dazzling in naval white.*

DEWEY
My great-grandfather, William Dewey, was a volunteer at the Battle of Lexington. My grandfather, Simeon Dewey, the embodiment of the old Puritan qualities, was a farmer on the virgin soil of Vermont. My father, Dr. Julius Dewey, was

15

a natural leader of men, with deep religious scruples. To his early influence — my mother dying when I was only five — I owe all that I have accomplished in the world.

Secretary Long *is at his desk, reviewing* Roosevelt's *orders.*

Long, *moans*
Oh my God.

calls out
Roosevelt! Where's Roosevelt?

Dewey, *continuing calmly*
When I assumed command of the Asiatic squadron some months ago, my files from Washington made only one reference to the Philippine Islands: a native rebellion was in progress there against Spain. No information of any sort was received that showed American interests to be affected.

reflectively
Of course, there are a great many more American interests than is generally known.

Long *is in a rage.* TR *stands near him, respectful, but firm.*

Long, *stamping* TR's *orders*
Revoked! Revoked! You can't go moving guns about the country and affecting Administration policy! Revoked! You have come near causing more of an explosion than happened to the *Maine!*

You order ammunition, which there is no means to move, to places where there is no means to store it! Your actions suggest that there has been a lack of attention here, which you are supplying!

Roosevelt, Roosevelt. Roosevelt, I love you as a father does a son, but the best fellow in the world (*patting him on the back*), and one with splendid capacities, is worse than useless if he lacks a cool head.

TR
I don't mean to interfere in foreign policy, sir, but I believe the cable to Commodore Dewey is an urgent matter. If we let the Spaniards take the initiative —

LONG, *reproving him wearily*
If there is war —

TR
If there is war, yes, they could send their Asian squadron off our west coast!

LONG, *uncertainly*
One doesn't want to appear in the light of being almost *over-prepared* for war . . . but the order to Dewey may stand. Still, it will need the President's approval.

TR, *delighted, to audience*
Long is just a dear.

stepping forward for a retrospective confidence
My chief usefulness in the Navy Department came about because, when I was Acting Secretary, I didn't hesitate to take responsibility and was willing to jeopardize my position. My rule always is: if in doubt, go ahead.

Lights up on LODGE, *in his office*

LODGE
I believe Theodore was never again permitted to serve as Acting Secretary.

Headlines appear.

**NAVAL COURT SAYS MINE EXPLODED UNDER
MAINE'S PORT SIDE**

WAR FEVER SWEEPS NATION

**PRESIDENT STILL HOPES FOR
PEACEFUL SETTLEMENT**

9

Office of Senator Lodge

TR storms in.

TR

Cabot! Have you heard what that white-livered cur, McKinley, has done? He has prepared two messages to Congress, one for war against Spain, and one for peace with Spain, and he doesn't know which one to send in! He's got no more backbone than a chocolate éclair!

Lodge, *grimly*

My God, if the situation in Cuba drags on through the summer, we shall go down in the greatest defeat at the polls ever known.

To bring on war for political reasons may be a crime (*boiling with indignation*) but to sacrifice the entire Republican party for a wrong policy is hardly less odious. We shall all go down in the wreck, senators and representatives alike!

10
The White House

The pleasant strains of a Schubert impromptu: White House guests nod to the music. H. H. KOHLSAAT, a Chicago newspaper publisher and influential friend of the President, speaks to the audience.

KOHLSAAT
In the first week of April I received a wire at my *Times-Herald* office in Chicago: "The President wants to see you." I laid down my publishing duties and went promptly, ever ready to help and advise, as I had done for years. When I arrived, there was a piano recital in the Blue Room. Mrs. McKinley was seated near the pianist, looking very frail and ill.

confidentially
Mrs. McKinley was subject to brief fainting spells, where she became rigid in her chair. If this happened at a White House dinner, the President would throw a napkin over her face and proceed as if nothing had happened. This discreet act spared her embarrassment later.

There never was a more devoted husband than President McKinley.

A presidential AIDE *summons* KOHLSAAT *in a whisper.*

AIDE
The President is trying to catch your eye.

McKINLEY *appears, motions to* KOHLSAAT.

McKinley

As soon as the pianist is through this piece, go to the Red Room door. I will join you.

Kohlsaat, *awaiting the President*

We sat on a crimson brocade lounge.

McKinley, *near tears*

I have been through a trying period. Mrs. McKinley has been in poorer health than usual. It seems to me I have not slept over three hours a night for two weeks. Congress is trying to drive us into war with Spain. The Spanish fleet is in Cuban waters, and we haven't enough ammunition on the east coast to fire a salute. (*he sobs*)

Kohlsaat

I put my hand on his shoulder and remained silent, as I thought the tension would be relieved by his tears. As he became calm, I tried to assure him that the country would back him in any course he should pursue. He finally looked up.

McKinley

Are my eyes very red? Do they look as if I've been crying?

Kohlsaat

Yes.

McKinley

But I must return to Mrs. McKinley at once. She is among strangers.

Kohlsaat

When you open the door to enter the room, blow your nose very hard and loud. It will force tears into your eyes and they will think that is what makes your eyes red.

20

MCKINLEY
Thanks, Kohlsaat.

KOHLSAAT, *to audience, gravely*
He acted on this suggestion, and it was no small blast.

MCKINLEY *honks his nose. Simultaneously, "Hail to the Chief"
strikes up.*

11
A Joint Session of the U.S. Senate and
House of Representatives

SENATORS and CONGRESSMEN *assemble for the President's
speech. The* PRESIDING OFFICER *gavels for quiet.* REPORT-
ERS *cluster at rear.*

CHIEF CLERK
The day of our Lord, April the eleventh, eighteen hundred and
ninety-eight. Will the Congress rise? Gentlemen: the President of the United States.

MCKINLEY *enters to polite applause. He waits until the* CONGRESS
is seated.

MCKINLEY
Gentlemen, in the name of humanity, in the name of civilization, in behalf of endangered American interests which give
us the right and the duty to speak and to act, the war in Cuba
must stop.

Applause

The only hope of relief and repose from a condition which can no longer be endured is the enforced pacification of Cuba. The insurrection by the Cuban natives and efforts by Spain to subdue it have carried destruction to every quarter of the island. It is not civilized warfare. It is extermination.

Against this abuse of the rights of war I have felt constrained on repeated occasions to enter the firm and earnest protest of this government.

Polite applause, and expressions of disparagement

Of the untried measures there remain only neutral intervention to end the war by imposing a rational compromise between the contestants; and intervention as the active ally of one party or another.

Cheers and applause

I speak not of forcible annexation, for that cannot be thought of. That, by our code of morality, would be criminal aggression.

Sustained applause. The LEGISLATORS *rise in affirmation.*

I have exhausted every effort to relieve the intolerable condition of affairs which is at our doors.

I now ask the Congress to empower the President to take measures to secure a full and final termination of hostilities in Cuba, to secure in the island the establishment of a stable government, and to use the military and naval forces of the United States as may be necessary for these purposes.

There is wild cheering. McKINLEY *waits for silence, then continues uncomfortably.*

Yesterday, and since the preparation of this message, official information was received by me that the latest decree of the Queen Regent of Spain directs the Spanish Commander in Cuba to proclaim a suspension of hostilities, the details of which have not been communicated to me.

This fact, and every other pertinent consideration, will, I am sure, have your just and careful attention in the solemn deliberations upon which you are about to enter. Prepared to execute every obligation imposed upon me by the Constitution, and the law, I await your action.

The scene explodes. All jump up, applauding, talking, waving their arms, shaking their fists. Frenzy hangs in the air.

REPORTER
The London *Times*: Members rushed up and down the aisles like madmen. Not for years has such a scene occurred.

REPORTER
The New York *World*: Our national duty is plain, simple, and imperative. Stop the nonsense! Stop the trifling! The army is ready. The navy is ready. The people are ready. Avenge the *Maine!*

REPORTER
The New York *Journal*: If we cannot have peace without fighting for it, let us fight and have it over with.

REPORTER
The New York *Sun*: The United States Government undertakes this high enterprise in the name of humanity and civilization, for the rights of brave men to liberty, for Cuba Libre. No war in history has been more righteous, or for a nobler cause.

There is a sudden shout. CONGRESS *has passed the war measure. The men cheer wildly, weep, embrace, sing "Dixie" and other war songs in voices hoarse with emotion. Headlines.*

CONGRESS DECLARES WAR WITH SPAIN

DISCLAIMS TERRITORIAL AMBITION
IN "WAR FOR HUMANITY"

PROMISES CUBA FOR CUBANS

A final REPORTER *offers a postmortem.*

REPORTER

The Boston *Transcript*: But Spain has backed down. Does she not offer the Cuban insurgents peace? Does she not offer them autonomy? Does she not offer to arbitrate the affair of the *Maine*? What more do we want?

Do we simply desire to show that we can wipe poor trembling Spain off the western hemisphere? Are we so eager to try our "flying squadron" and our new destroyers that we will not let this pitifully weak antagonist back down?

Our Congress is driving on like a rush of stampeded bulls. But why are we going to war?

Congratulating each other, the LEGISLATORS *straggle off. One stays behind, lighting a pipe. He shares a bit of* realpolitik *with the audience.*

SENATOR

I think possibly the President could have worked out the business without war. But the current was too strong. The demagogues were too numerous. And the fall elections were too near.

Headlines

IMMEDIATE MOBILIZATION ORDERED
CALL FOR 125,000 VOLUNTEERS

Gay sounds of "There'll Be a Hot Time in the Old Town To-night" and the tramp of marching feet

12

A New York Club

Two aging CLUBMEN *watch mobilization from the window.*

FIRST CLUBMAN
God! I believe the whole country would enlist if need be. Where I sit in the Knickerbocker Club . . . sports, loafers, athletes, dandies . . . raised in cotton wool, raised in a rose garden — and it's just a little club — why, forty have gone already!

SECOND CLUBMAN
You don't say!

FIRST CLUBMAN
Eleven per cent of the club. (*mistily*) Of course, like the old fool I am, I long to go in myself . . .

They chuckle, a little sadly. Mobilization sounds intensify.

The Senate Cloakroom

FIRST SENATOR
I really think Roosevelt is going mad. The President asked him twice, as a personal favor, to stay in the Navy Department, but Theodore had to volunteer for the cavalry. He is wild to hack and hew. It is really sad.

SECOND SENATOR
Of course this ends his political career for good. Even Cabot says so.

FIRST SENATOR, *shrugs*
Of course.

14

The Rough Rider Recruiting Office

Lieutenant Colonel ROOSEVELT *sits behind a table in the field attire of the U.S. Cavalry. A well-dressed* YOUNG MAN *enters, carrying fine luggage.*

TR
Name?

YOUNG MAN
My name is Dudley Dean, Colonel Roosevelt, sir.

TR
Home state?

DEAN
New Hampshire, sir.

TR
Education?

DEAN
I went to Harvard, sir.

TR, *suddenly jumping up and shaking his hand*
Why yes, I know you! You were the best quarterback who ever
played on the Harvard team! You're the kind of man we want!

DEAN, *thrilled*
Really?

TR, *a further recognition*
Yes, you're the man who saved the day for Harvard in the
great game with Yale! I'm a Harvard man myself.

abruptly serious
Now, Dean, we have Southwest cowboys and hunters in the
regiment. They can ride wild horses and handle a rifle moving.
There will be disagreeable work as well as dangerous. I'm glad
to have you college men, but once signed up there can be no
backing out. Are you with us?

DEAN, *signing deliriously*
Yessir!!

TR
Attention!

They exchange salutes. TR's *handpicked* VOLUNTEERS *march
across, chanting,* "To Hell with Spain, Remember the Maine."

*Their types range from cowpoke to history scholar to society
swell. The contrasts in dress, gear, and demeanor are extreme.
TR shouts orders and encouragement. Young* DEAN *falls into
line at the end.*

15

Manila Bay

*It is midnight. The rumbling of a ship's engine is heard.
On the bridge of the flagship Olympia, we discern the imposing form of Commodore* DEWEY. *Dateline appears.*

MAY 1, 1898

DEWEY, *in a hushed voice*
With all lights masked and gun crews at the guns, the squadron
steamed quietly toward the entrance of Manila Bay. We
passed Corregidor. The high land on either side loomed up out
of the darkness. A light shower passed. Heavy clouds drifting
across the sky obscured the new moon.

At 4:00 A.M. coffee was served to the men. We were heading
slowly toward the city of Manila, awaiting the object for which
we had made our arduous preparations.

At 5:15, in the misty haze of the tropical dawn, the Spanish
squadron opened a hasty and inaccurate fire. They were seven
ships to our six. We were superior in class of vessel and arma-
ments.

raising his voice over the sound of firing
It was thirty-six years since I was first under fire. In the Civil

War, I was in the Battle of New Orleans with Admiral Farragut.

He was my ideal of the naval officer: urbane, decisive, indomitable. Whenever since I have been in a difficult situation, I have asked myself, "What would Farragut do?"

Spanish naval fire illumines DEWEY *in a spectacular light. He raises his arm, then drops it decisively.*

Fire when ready, Gridley!

Furious firing erupts. Headlines.

DEWEY HERO AT MANILA!

**SPANISH SHIPS BLOWN UP,
SUNK AND BURNED!**

OUR SHIPS UNHARMED

6 AMERICANS INJURED, NONE KILLED

ENEMY ADMITS LOSS OF 618

SPAIN'S EASTERN FLEET UTTERLY DESTROYED

16

Office of Senator Lodge

The correspondence flows on, almost in the nature of a conversation, undisturbed by shot and shell.

LODGE
Dear Theodore. I think I can tell you, in confidence, but in absolute certainty, that the Administration is grasping the

whole policy at last. They mean to send not less than twenty thousand men to the Philippines.

As to Cuba, I am in no sort of hurry. Our troops are fresh and raw. They ought to be hardened up. All this takes time. We ought to take Porto Rico and then close in on Cuba. The one point where haste is needed is in the Philippines. Let us get the outlying things first.

Headlines

ARMY ASSEMBLING IN FLORIDA
FOR CUBAN ASSAULT

ROOSEVELT'S ROUGH RIDERS "RARIN' TO GO"

WASHINGTON POSTPONES INVASION

LONG DELAY FORESEEN

17

The Embarkment Site at Tampa

TR's demoralized men grumble in the background.

TR, *wild with frustration*
The confusion is incredible! It took three days to get the troops on the transports, in sweltering heat. Then we receive word from Washington not to start!

I can't speak publicly — I'd be court-martialed if I did — but, Cabot, please! Tell the President just what is going on here!

They unloaded the horses for the simple reason that they began to die. We'd be glad to go on all fours if we had to, but it is hard upon the cavalry to leave behind their horses. Please, old man! I know what a fight you have on strictly the line of your own duties — you *must* get Hawaii, you must prevent peace talk until we get Porto Rico and the Philippines. But please do try, old man, to see that we get out of this sewer, and over to Cuba!

Headlines

HOUSE READY TO ANNEX HAWAII
CHANGE OF SENTIMENT CAUSED BY WAR
NEED FOR MID-OCEAN COALING STATION SEEN

18
Office of Senator Lodge

LODGE

Good news! The Hawaiian business is practically settled. It passed the House by a large majority. In the Senate just now we are face-to-face with a dogged filibuster led by — you can imagine who —

TR, *mutters from across the stage at Tampa*
Pettigrew, the obnoxious swine.

LODGE

Pettigrew, naturally. But the Senate can't hold out very long. (*elated*) If I am not utterly mistaken, the Administration is fully committed to the large policy we both desire. The drift of public opinion in favor of an imperial policy seems absolutely overwhelming. We'll sweep the country on the issue!

19

Somewhere in the Gulf of Mexico

The ROUGH RIDERS cheer joyously and shout raucous shouts
— "Cuba, here we come!" and "Give 'em hell in Havana!"
The band strikes up "The Girl I Left Behind Me." Head-
lines.

ARMY LEAVES KEY WEST AT DAYBREAK

CUBAN INVASION NOW IN EARNEST

TR leans dreamily against the deck rail. His men sing.

ROUGH RIDERS
>The hour was sad, I left the maid,
>A ling'ring farewell taking.
>Her sighs and tears my steps delayed,
>I thought her heart was breaking.
>In hurried words her name I blessed,
>I breath'd the vows that bind me,
>And to my heart in anguish pressed,
>The girl I left behind me.

VOLUNTEER, approaching ROOSEVELT
How do you feel, sir, now that we're finally underway?

TR, warmly
It is a great historical expedition, and I am thrilled that I am
part of it.

TR looks into the sunset. Tears glisten on his cheeks. The MEN
sing softly, as lights dim to black.

20

Mr. Dooley Explains the War to Mr. Hennessey

MR. DOOLEY's *saloon, Archey Road, the Sixth Ward, Chi-cago.* MR. DOOLEY *and* MR. HENNESSEY, *fictional creatures of newspaper columnist Finley Peter Dunne, are at their usual places —* MR. HENNESSEY *at a small table nursing a beer;* MR. DOOLEY *behind the bar, studying the newspaper spread before him. There is a long, reflective silence.*

MR. HENNESSEY
Well, Mr. Dooley, how goes th' war?

MR. DOOLEY
Splendid, thank ye, Hinnissy, fine, fine. It makes me hear-rt throb with pride that I'm a citizen iv th' Sixth Wa-ard.

thumping his newspaper
Well, sir, I didn't vote f'r Mack — that's Mack-Kinley, Hin-nissy — but I'm with him now. I had me doubts whether he was th' gr-reatest military janius iv th' cinchry, but they'se no question about it, Hinnissy. Th' first gr-reat land battle iv th' war has been fought an' won.

MR. HENNESSEY
Where was that, Mr. Dooley? Lord save us, but where was that?

MR. DOOLEY
Three thousand ar-rmy mules. Hinnissy, bruk fr'm the' corral where they had thim tied up, atin' thistles, an' med a desp-rate charge on th' camp at Tampa. They dayscinded like a whur-rlwind, dhrivin' th' astonished throops before thim, an' thin charged back again, completin' their errand iv desthruction.

At th' las' account th' brave sojers was climbin' threes an' tillygraft poles.

Th' gallant mules was led by a most courageous jackass, an' 'tis undhersthud that me friend Mack will appint him a brigadier gin'ral. He's th' biggest jackass in Tampa today, not exciptin' th' army cinsor. An' I doubt if they'se a bigger wan in Wash'n'ton. Annyhow, they'll know how to reward him. They know a jackass whin they see wan.

Up to this time th' on'y hero kilt on th' Spanish side was a jackass that poked an ear above th' batthries f'r to hear what was goin' on. "Behold," says our gin'ral, "th' insolince iv th' foe," he says. "For-rm in line iv battle, an' hur-rl death an' desthruction at yon Castilyan gin'ral."

"Wait," says an officer. "It may be wan iv our own men. It looks like th' sicrety iv . . ." "Hush!" says th' commander. "It can't be an American jackass, or he'd speak," he says. "Fire on him!"

Shot afther shot fell round th' intrepid ass. But he remained firm till th' dinnymite boat *Vesoovyus* fired three hundherd an' forty thousand pounds iv gum cotton at him, an' the poor critter smothered to death.

What's needed to carry on this war as it goes today, Hinnissy, is an ar-rmy iv jacks an' mules. Th' ordhers fr'm Wash'n'ton is perfectly comprehensible to a jackass, but they don't mane annything to a poor foolish man. What we need, Hinnissy, is what Tim Horgan calls th' esprite th' corpse, an' we'll only have it whin th' mules begins to move.

MR. HENNESSEY, *doubtfully*
But we're a gr-reat people.

MR. DOOLEY
We ar-re, Hinnissy, we ar-re that. An' th' best iv it is, we know
we ar-re.

21

The Front

*Lights flash, guns crash, and smoke fills the stage. Through
the haze of battle emerge war tableaux.*

BLOODY LAS GUASIMAS — FIRST BATTLE IN CUBA

*We see "*FIGHTING JOE*" WHEELER, a Confederate general re-
activated in the crisis.*

WHEELER, *exultantly, peering into the distance*
We've got the Yankees on the run!

YOUNG OFFICER
The Yankees, sir?

WHEELER
I mean the Spaniards!

Naval guns boom. Screams of the dying in the background.

VICTORY AT SANTIAGO!
Spain's Western Fleet Destroyed

Cheers from American side. We see a NAVAL OFFICER.

NAVAL OFFICER
Don't cheer, men. Those poor devils are dying!

A crescendo of artillery

ROUGH RIDERS STORM SAN JUAN HILL

 R<small>OOSEVELT</small> *appears in a blaze of light, followed by his* M<small>EN</small>.

TR
  Charge!

R<small>OUGH</small> R<small>IDERS</small>
  CHARGE!!!

Philippine band music is heard.

DEWEY ASKS FILIPINO AID TO OUST SPAIN

D<small>EWEY</small> *towers over a* G<small>ENERAL</small> *of the Philippine insurgent army, who wreathes him with garlands and kisses him on the cheeks.*

G<small>ENERAL</small>, *weeping*
  Viva Dewey! Viva los Americanos! Viva la independencia filipina!

D<small>EWEY</small>, *patting him on the head*
  In my opinion, these people are far superior in intelligence and more capable of self-government than the natives of Cuba, and I am familiar with both races.

Shouts of "Viva!" and "Libertad!"

Office of Senator Lodge

LODGE, *in unaccustomed hilarity*
Theodore! Perhaps among the alarms and excursions of your active war you may like to turn your thoughts to something frivolous. It will amuse you more than anything that has happened.

A certain Captain (*checking the name in the newspaper*) Glass, on the U.S.S. *Charleston*, stopped at the Island of Guam on his way to the Philippines and proceeded to shell the forts. The Spanish governor in full uniform came out and said that he regretted that he had no powder with which to return the salute.

Glass replied that this was war — the Spanish governor expressed surprise — whereupon Glass took him prisoner with the entire government and Spanish army, consisting of fifty-four men, and carried them off to Manila. But the most amusing feature of the whole thing was that Glass found on this remote island an American resident whom he appointed governor. So this American was made governor and that island is ours today.

he laughs
I believe that in every spot of the world there is an American resident ready to become governor. (*roars with laughter*)

The Trenches Outside Santiago

Firing and explosions tapering off. ROUGH RIDERS *lying about, ill and wounded. The lights steady to reveal TR, in battle disarray, peering darkly from a trench.*

TR

Cabot, old man, not since the campaign of Crassus against the Parthians has there been so criminally incompetent a general as Shafter. He never came within three miles of the line! He was too fat to get to the front! The battle simply fought itself.

The siege guns have not been landed. The mortars have not been started from the landing place. The men are half-starved and in tatters. Sick men in high fever lie on soggy blankets without so cheap a comfort as rice or sugar. The mismanagement is beyond belief! It is grotesque!

climbs out and stretches rapturously
I never expected to come through. How I have escaped I know not. We lost one quarter of our men. I have been at the extreme front of the firing line. I sleep in drenching rain and drink putrid water. I have not taken off my shoes even! The fighting has been very hard.

fondly surveying his ravaged men
These men would follow me anywhere now. Why, the gallant fellows struggle back to me from the hospital just as soon as their wounds are healed or the dysentery lets up a little.

After we made the break in the Spanish line and took the three hills outside Santiago —

Two of the MEN *raise their heads and feebly cry, "Give 'em hell!"* —

General Wheeler visited us at the front and told me to keep myself in readiness as it might be decided to fall back. I answered, "Well, General, I really don't know whether we would obey an order to fall back. If we have to move out of here at all," I said, "I should be inclined to make the rush in the right direction!"

modestly
Now General Wheeler says he intends to recommend me for the Medal of Honor. Naturally, I should like to have it.

LODGE *appears at his desk.*

TR, *turning to him*
Well, old man, even if I go of yellow fever tomorrow, I am satisfied.

LODGE, *anxiously*
Oh, Theodore!

TR
At least I leave my children an honorable name. But if I do go, Cabot, old man, please see what you can do about pushing through the Medal of Honor for me?

LODGE, *rising*
We've been living with our hearts in our mouths about you.

TR
I feel as strong as a bull moose!

LODGE
Thank God you are safe.

TR, *nostalgically*
Did I tell you I killed a Spaniard with my own hand?

LODGE
You have no idea of your popularity here! You are one of *the* conspicuous heroes of the fight. Everybody thinks so.

TR
Probably I told you.

LODGE
You can have pretty much anything you want at this moment. What I want for you is the Senate, but the newspapers are nominating you for governor of New York. That might lead you to the Senate next winter. Or you can certainly go to Congress if you want to.

Oh! I was all wrong about your going into the war, and you were all right! (*he embraces* TR *impulsively*)

TR, *fervently*
It was great luck — in the biggest thing since the Civil War — to get into the fighting. I'll always be thankful for it.

A Sousa march is heard, and distant cheering. Headlines.

NATIVES WELCOME LIBERATORS
TRIUMPHAL MARCH IN PORTO RICO
FILIPINOS PROCLAIM INDEPENDENCE
AUGUST 12, 1898
S P A I N   G I V E S   U P !
HOSTILITIES SUSPENDED PENDING PEACE TREATY
YIELDS CUBA, PORTO RICO, GUAM,
AND CONTROL OF MANILA

24

A Victory Rally in the Streets of New York

Cheering and march music grow louder. A holiday CROWD
fills the stage. A SPEAKER *on the platform shouts over the
noise.*

SPEAKER
It has been a splendid little war, begun with the highest motives — carried on with magnificent intelligence and spirit —
favored by that fortune which loves the brave. It is now to be
concluded with the fine good nature which is, after all, the
distinguishing trait of our American character.

A portly BUSINESSMAN *steps toward the podium.*

BUSINESSMAN
The first and paramount obligation connected with the war
is the moral duty growing out of it. Now, I might dwell upon
the value of the Philippine Islands. I might speak of the en-
larged trade which their fertility and richness offer, when
brought under the peaceful sway of civilizing development.
There is no code of ethics which excludes consideration of the
commercial interest involved in our public policy. And when
the moral mandate and the material interest completely blend,
the policy is doubly wise and the duty doubly commanding.

DEWEY — *now Admiral Dewey* — *appears on another platform.
The* CROWD *rushes over. Majestically, he beams down on them.
A* PHOTOGRAPHER *takes his picture;* NEWSPAPERMEN *push for-
ward. The band plays.*

CROWD, *singing along*
        Oh dewy was the morning,
        Upon the first of May,

And Dewey was the admiral,
Down in Manila Bay.
And dewy were the regent's eyes,
Them orbs of royal blue,
And dew we feel discouraged?
I dew not think we dew!

DEWEY

I want to convey to the people of New York City heartfelt thanks for this magnificent reception. When the great metropolis of this country shows such enthusiasm, the nation is safe.

to REPORTERS

Oh, you don't want to take down my speech. I couldn't make a speech worth reporting.

REPORTER

Won't you say something about your great victory, sir?

DEWEY, *thinks a moment*

If I were a religious man, and I hope I am, I should say that the hand of God was in it.

An unsavory New York politician steps up. This is Boss RICHARD CROKER, *King of Tammany.*

CROKER

Admiral Dewey, we want to run you for President on the Democratic ticket.

The CROWD *applauds.*

DEWEY, *laughing no, but meaning yes*

Oh no sir, Mr. Croker. I am a navy man, and I don't want any part of it.

CROKER
  Admiral, we're gonna run you, and meanwhile, don't you say
  nothin'.

DEWEY, *to* CROWD, *gaily*
  There's a man who runs Tammany Hall and owns New York
  City, and he tells me not to protest.

Laughter

  I have said that nothing would induce me to be a candidate
  for the presidency.

Chanting now, "We want Dewey!"

CROKER, *shouts a good-natured warning*
  Admiral, we're going to run you.

DEWEY
  Many assurances have come to me from my countrymen that
  I would be acceptable as a candidate for the presidency. If the
  American people want me for this high office, I shall be only
  too willing to serve them. What citizen would refuse it?

Cheers, DEWEY *fends off a persistent* REPORTER.

  I think I have said enough at this time. Possibly too much.

On the other platform, a GENERAL *begins to speak.*

GENERAL
  My friends, war is gradually changing its character. It once
  involved the lust of conquest, the slaughter of the vanquished,
  the violation of virtue. But the army among Anglo-Saxon peoples is no longer a mere instrument of destruction. It is promoting law, order, and civilization.

43

Cowboy *yelps. Some* Rough Riders *march on, destroying the general's moment. The* Crowd *shouts, "Teddy, Teddy — We want Teddy!" and "Roosevelt for governor!"* TR *appears, swinging his hat.*

TR
As for politics, I haven't had a moment to think of them.

Laughter

I am happy to be in the favor of the good people of New York. But it is not very long since they thought I compared unfavorably with Caligula. (*They love him. He can do no wrong.*) And I don't know how to get on with New York politicians.

The Crowd *howls its delight.*

If I were a rich man, I could go into national politics, because the average New York boss (*with eyebrows raised he looks around for bosses, then continues in mock secrecy*) is quite willing to allow you to do what you wish in such trivial matters as war, and the acquisition of Porto Rico and Hawaii, provided you don't interfere with the really vital questions, such as giving out contracts for cartage in the customhouse, and interfering with the appointment of street sweepers. (*grimacing*) But state politics . . .

Laughter

Still, if I am nominated, I shall work like a beaver and do everything I can do to be elected.

The Rough Riders *cheer and whistle. A* Clergyman *begins to speak.*

44

Fellow Christians: Can anyone doubt that God, with infinite wisdom and skill, is training the Anglo-Saxon for the final competition of the races? Is there room for reasonable doubt that the Anglo-Saxon, as the great representative of Christianity and liberty, is divinely commissioned to be his brother's keeper? Is there room for reasonable doubt that the Anglo-Saxon race is destined to dispossess many weaker races, assimilate others, and mold the remainder until it has spread itself across the earth, and anglo-saxonized mankind? Let us pray.

25
Tomlinson Hall, Indianapolis

Headlines

SEPTEMBER 16, 1898

ALBERT J. BEVERIDGE OPENS INDIANA REPUBLICAN CAMPAIGN

RISING YOUNG ATTORNEY GIVES TALK OF CENTURY

WILD ENTHUSIASM GREETS STIRRING WORDS

BEVERIDGE *is a dashing figure on the rise in American politics. He is in his mid-thirties, a man of effortless grace and charm, gifted with phenomenal powers of oratory.*

BEVERIDGE
In 1789, the flag of the Republic waved over four million souls

45

in thirteen states and their savage territory, which stretched to the Mississippi, to Canada, and to the Floridas. The timid souls of the day said that no new territory was needed, and, for an hour, they were right.

But Jefferson, through whose intellect the centuries marched; Jefferson, whose blood was Saxon; Jefferson, the first imperialist of the Republic! — Jefferson acquired that imperial territory which swept from the Mississippi to the mountains, from Texas to the British possessions, and the march of the flag began.

Those who denied the power of free institutions to expand urged every argument and more that we hear today; but the people's judgment approved the command of their blood, and the march of the flag went on!

Applause

Under Monroe, Florida came under the dominion of the Republic, and the march of the flag went on.

Then Texas responded to the bugle call of liberty, and the march of the flag went on.

At last, we waged war with Mexico, and the flag swept over the Southwest, over peerless California, past the Golden Gate to Oregon, and from ocean to ocean its folds of glory blazed.

And now — William McKinley plants the flag over all the islands of the seas, outposts of commerce, citadels of national security, and the march of the flag goes on!

Cheering. BEVERIDGE *continues with quiet derision.*

46

But does the opposition say that, unlike other lands, these lands of Spain are not contiguous? The ocean does not separate us from the lands of our duty and desire. The ocean joins us. Steam joins us. Electricity joins us. The very elements are in league with our destiny. The Philippines not contiguous? Our navy will make them (*biting off the syllables*) contiguous! And American speed, American guns, American heart and brain and nerve will keep them contiguous forever!

Applause and cheering

Hawaii is ours. Porto Rico is ours. The stars and stripes of glory will float over the Philippines. Will the American people accept, or reject, the gifts of events? Will they rise, as lifts their soaring destiny? Or will the American people, for the first time, doubt their mission, and halt the ceaseless march of free institutions?

Cries of "No, No!"

My friends, this question is deeper than any question of party politics. Deeper even than any question of constitutional power. It is elemental. It is racial. God has not been preparing the English-speaking and Teutonic peoples for a thousand years for nothing but vain and idle self-admiration. No! He has made us the master organizers of the world, to establish system where chaos reigns. He has given us the spirit of progress to overwhelm the forces of reaction throughout the earth. He has made us adept in government that we may administer government among savage and senile peoples. Were it not for such a force as this, the world would relapse into barbarism. And of all our race, He has marked the American people as His chosen nation to finally lead in the regeneration of the world.

47

Blind is he who sees not the hand of God in events so vast, so harmonious, so benign. Now, on the threshold of our career as the first power of the earth, the golden future is before us. The world calls us. God's command is upon us. Fellow Americans, we are God's chosen people!

Tumultuous applause. "America, the Beautiful" cascades from the organ.

26

Mr. Dooley Ponders the Fruits of Victory

Mr. Dooley and Mr. Hennessey are hunched over the counter of the saloon, pints of beer at their elbows. Dooley chews a cigar. They are silent awhile, deep in cards.

Dooley

Well, Hinnissy, it's over now. An' I'm glad iv it. The war, Hinnissy, has been a gr-reat sthrain on me. To think iv th' suffrin' I've endured! Ye heerd iv Teddy Rosenfelt plungin' into ambus-cades. But did ye hear iv Martin Dooley, th' man behind th' guns, four thousan' miles behind thim, an' willin' to be further?

They shake their heads somberly.

They ar-re no bokays f'r me . . . Someday Hinnissy, justice'll be done me. An' whin th' story iv th' gr-reat battle is written, they'll print th' kilt, th' wounded, th' missin', an' th' seryously disturbed. An' thim thet have bore thimsilves well an' bravely an' paid th' taxes an' faced th' deadly newspapers without flinchin' 'll be advanced six pints an' given a chanst to tur-rn jack f'r th' game.

He turns a card with emphasis. They drink.

But me wurruk ain't over jus' because Mack has inded th' war. You an' me, Hinnissy, has got to bring on this here Anglo-Saxon alliance. They're a lot iv Anglo-Saxons in this country, Hinnissy. There must be as manny as two in Boston. They'se wan up in Maine. Teddy Rosenfelt is an Anglo-Saxon. An' I'm an Anglo-Saxon. Th' name iv Dooley has been th' proudest Anglo-Saxon name in th' County Roscommon f'r many years. Me ol' friend Domingo will march at the head iv th' Eyetalian Anglo-Saxons whin th' time comes. There ar-re twinty thousan' Rooshian Jews in th' Sivinth Ward. They'd be a tur-rble thing f'r anny inimy iv th' Anglo-Saxon alliance to face.

I tell ye, Hinnissy, whin th' Sons iv Sweden, an' th' Circle Francaize, an' th' Pollacky Benivolent Society, an' th' Benny Brith, an' th' Afro-Americans an' th' other Anglo-Saxons begin f'r to raise their Anglo-Saxon battle cry, it'll be all day with th' eight or nine people in th' wurruld that has th' misfortune iv not bein' brought up Anglo-Saxons.

They drink.

HENNESSEY
Is Mack-Kinley an Anglo-Saxon?

DOOLEY
Mack? (*slams his beer mug on the counter*) He's wan iv th' hottest Anglo-Saxons that iver come out iv Anglo-Saxony!

HENNESSEY
I hear he's in town. Did ye see him?

DOOLEY
Faith, I did not. I may niver see him. I may go to me grave

without settin' an eye on th' wan man besides mesilf that don't know what th' furrin policy iv th' United States is goin' to be.

They lapse into silence, sipping their beer.

HENNESSEY

An' what do you think ought to be done with th' fruits iv victhry, Mr. Dooley?

DOOLEY

I dinnaw, Hinnissy. Wan iv th' worst things about th' war is th' puzzles it's made f'r our poor, tired heads. Whin I wint into it, I thought all I'd have to do was to set up here behind th' bar with a good tin-cint see-gar in me teeth an' toss dinnymite bombs into th' hated city iv Havana. But look at me now. Ivry night, whin I'm countin' up th' cash, I'm askin' mesilf, what shud I do with th' Ph'lippeens? Oh, what shud I do with thim? I can't annex thim because I don't know where they ar-re. I can't let go iv thim because somewan else'll take thim if I do. They ar-re eight thousan' iv them islands, an' me bedroom's crowded now with me an' th' bed. How can I take thim in? An' yet, 'twud br-reak me hear-rt to think iv givin' people I niver see or heerd tell iv back to other people I don't know. An' if I don't take thim, Schwartzmeister down th' sthreet, that has half me thrade already, will grab thim sure.

An' yet, Hinnissy, I'm all alone in th' wurruld. Ivrybody else has made up his mind what to do about th' Ph'lippeens. It ain't that I'm afraid iv not doin' th' r-right thing in th' end, Hinnissy, but 'tis th' annoyance in th' manetime.

HENNESSEY

I know what I'd do if I was Mack. I'd hist a flag over th' Ph'lippeens, an' I'd take in th' whole lot iv thim. (*unbottling the jingo in his thin soul*) I'm fer takin' thim in.

DOOLEY, *astonished*
> An' yet, 'tis not more thin two months since ye larned whether they were islands or canned goods.

HENNESSEY, *emphatic*
> Hang on to thim. What we've got, we must hold!

HENNESSEY *nods with unaccustomed assurance.* DOOLEY *shakes his head dubiously.*

ACT TWO

1

A Meeting Hall in Boston

GEORGE BOUTWELL, *former Massachusetts governor, now eighty years of age, is indignantly addressing his fellow patricians.*

BOUTWELL
It is useless for the President to disclaim imperialism when we are red-handed in the very act!

Applause. Shouts of "Right!" and "Yes!"

I daresay there is no intention to withdraw even from Cuba until American influences shall dominate.

Cries of "No!"

It is the old spirit of slavery, and its disguise is the thinnest!

Sustained applause. Headlines.

52

LEADING CITIZENS PROTEST "IMPERIALISM"
FORMER MASSACHUSETTS GOVERNOR BOUTWELL
HEADS NEW ORGANIZATION

BOUTWELL, *reading*
Name: The Anti-Imperialist League.

Object: To oppose the acquisition of the Philippine Islands.

Resolved: That a war begun as an unselfish endeavor to fulfill a duty to humanity in Cuba must not be perverted into a war of conquest —

VOICES
Good! Fine! Yes!

BOUTWELL
That our first duty is to cure the evils in our own country, to protect the rights of men within our own borders — the colored race in the South, and the Indians in the West —

There is applause.

For we hold with Abraham Lincoln that "no man is good enough to govern another without his consent."

Great applause

All in favor say "Aye."

A roar of approval, followed by "The Battle Hymn of the Republic." Headlines.

CARL SCHURZ NAMED A VICE-PRESIDENT
OF ANTI-IMPERIALIST LEAGUE
URGES DEFEAT OF PEACE TREATY

53

Sounds of the "Battle Hymn" die as SCHURZ *steps forward to applause. He is nearly seventy. He speaks with a slight German accent. In his eyes and bearing, we see flashes of the young revolutionary of 1848.*

SCHURZ

We old anti-slavery men have in our days seen darker situations than this. When the popular conscience concerning slavery seemed absolutely dead, it suddenly rose up in its might and did not rest until slavery was wiped out.

Let us recapitulate. We go to war with Spain in behalf of an oppressed colony of hers. We solemnly proclaim this to be a war — not of conquest! — God forbid! — but of liberation and humanity. We invade the Spanish colony of the Philippines, destroy the Spanish fleet, and invite the cooperation of the Filipino insurgents, under their leader Aguinaldo, against Spain — all the while permitting them to believe that in case of victory they will be free and independent.

By active fighting the insurgent Philippine army of some thirty thousand men gets control of a large part of the interior country. But when we have captured Manila and have no further use for our Filipino allies, our President directs that behind their backs a treaty be made with Spain, transferring what is called Spanish "sovereignty" to the United States for a consideration of twenty million dollars.

The sovereignty thus acquired may well be defined — in Abraham Lincoln's words — as being like a soup made by boiling the shadow of the breastbone of a pigeon that had been starved to death.

Nothing in our times has discredited the name of republic in the civilized world as much as the Dreyfus outrage in France and our conquest furor in America — and our conquest furor more, because from us the world hoped more.

VOICES
   Shame!

SCHURZ, *nodding*
   Atrocious, is it not?

Shouts of agreement

Now look at this calmly if you can. We are now being asked to agree to a treaty which takes away from the inhabitants of those islands their right to their own country. The matter is near its decision, but not yet decided. The treaty is not yet ratified by the Senate.

And no wonder it finds opposition in the Senate! A peace treaty? This is no peace treaty at all. It is a treaty with half a dozen bloody wars in its belly. And I say that treaty should be bitterly and determinedly opposed!

Sustained applause. The "Battle Hymn" starts again. SCHURZ *and* BOUTWELL *sing the words, nostalgic for the idealism of their youth.*

2

From the Pages of the Boston *Herald*

A newspaper advertisement appears. The voice of a REPORTER *is heard reading the copy.*

The Boston *Herald*

> *an advertisement*
>
> Should the United States Expand?
>
> ANDREW CARNEGIE
> says
> NO!
>
> *in this week's number of the*
> SATURDAY EVENING POST

An EDITOR *of the* HERALD *steps forward.*

EDITOR
The Boston *Herald*. An editorial. "It would seem that Mr. Andrew Carnegie has taken the anti-expansionist fever harder than anyone else in the country.

"Mr. Carnegie is a vice-president of the Anti-Imperialist League and is its primary source of funds. The latest report is to the effect that this man, a lifelong Republican, has formally abandoned the Party in disgust with what has been done under its administration. Mr. Carnegie is charged with promising aid to Democrat William Jennings Bryan in next year's presidential campaign.

"Here indeed is one of the strange mutations of politics. There is proof in it, if confirmed, of an impaired, if not unsettled, judgment in the great manufacturer."

3
The Fifth Avenue Mansion of Andrew Carnegie

In Carnegie's handsome study, two vice-presidents of the Anti-Imperialist League, HERBERT MYRICK *and* EDWARD ATKINSON, *hover about seeking funds from the great man.* MYRICK *is editor and publisher of a string of influential farm journals;* ATKINSON, *a pamphleteer in a dozen reform causes, is a strong-willed and eccentric Boston businessman. From their briefcases they unload pamphlets and petition forms.*

CARNEGIE, *in shirtsleeves, is keeping two male* SECRETARIES *and his* CASHIER *busy. He dictates rapidly, with a distinct Scottish burr.*

CARNEGIE
To Secretary of State John Hay, State Department, Washington — as follows: My dear Colonel. Pay no attention to rumors about Bryan and your faithful servant.

dropping his voice
My friend, the President does not know he is drifting to the devil! Strictly confidential between ourselves, he sees only one judge of the Supreme Court, and he is an untrustworthy adviser. Strictly now, my friend, between ourselves, I advise you

to counsel the President to send for the other judges. There is not one of them that will not tell the President that he is making the mistake of his lifetime taking the Philippines.

suddenly booming
If the President awakes from the abyss into which he is about to plunge, he will thank me for being his best friend—

FIRST SECRETARY, *breathless*
Sorry, Mr. Carnegie, sir (*puzzled*) "awakes" from the abyss, sir?

CARNEGIE, *nodding vigorously, missing the point*
As deep as hell!

The SECOND SECRETARY *has been opening mail. He hands* CARNEGIE *a sheaf of letters to look through.*

MYRICK
Did you see yesterday's Chicago *Times-Herald?*

ATKINSON
No.

CARNEGIE, *hands a letter to* CASHIER
Send him five hundred dollars.

MYRICK
It is practically McKinley's personal mouthpiece, you know, and it has made the sensational announcement that it is against annexation!

ATKINSON, *fairly dancing*
We are going to win hands down!

58

CARNEGIE, *pleased*
So we are.

handing letter to SECOND SECRETARY
Tell him no.

ATKINSON *shows* MYRICK *a petition.*

ATKINSON
Before mid-January there will be anywhere from two to four million signatures on these in Washington.

MYRICK, *incredulous*
Four million!

ATKINSON
Eight million! But I want to be moderate. I've drawn up this pamphlet — I've nearly broken down in the rush preparing it —

CARNEGIE, *handing* SECOND SECRETARY *a letter*
Tell him I can do nothing until I return from Washington. What's that, Atkinson?

MYRICK
"The Cost of a National Crime"? (*looks through pamphlet*)

ATKINSON
Twenty-five thousand copies, seven thousand to clergymen.

CARNEGIE, *approving*
The clergy are becoming aroused.

ATKINSON
The pamphlet appeals to the moral sense. (*smoothly*) I've incurred obligations for three hundred dollars or more . . .

CARNEGIE
I've spent fifteen thousand myself.

ATKINSON
I need five hundred dollars for postage. Don't do it if you don't approve.

CARNEGIE, *waving him to the* CASHIER
Take care of Mr. Atkinson.

ATKINSON
I feel mean coming to you again . . .

CARNEGIE, *dictating loudly*
When a jellyfish wishes to conceal its whereabouts (FIRST SECRETARY *leaps for his pencil*) it does so by ebullitions of blubber, and this is what people say the President is doing — following public clamor, and not speaking his convictions. Yet if one American soldier's blood is spilled shooting down insurgents in the Philippines, the President shall be like another "Mac" . . .

declaiming
"He shall sleep no more!"

The BUTLER *puts his head in.*

BUTLER
Mr. Carnegie, sir, the men from the newspapers —

CARNEGIE
Let them wait! And where is the whisky?

BUTLER *leaves.*

60

Myrick! How may I be of service to you?

MYRICK
We —

CARNEGIE
Where do the farmers stand? Abreast of labor on this issue?

MYRICK
They —

CARNEGIE
Labor has taken alarm. On Sunday the New York labor groups will hold a protest at the Brooklyn Academy of Music.

MYRICK, *politely*
Oh? Who is speaking?

ATKINSON
Samuel Gompers.

CARNEGIE
Gompers and I will save the nation! (*chortling*) Business and labor, hmmm?

BUTLER *enters with bottle of whisky.* CARNEGIE *seizes it delightedly.*

The very thing!

dictating
My friend, sorry to hear of your indisposition. I send you whisky from the Queen's vat — the lot I refurnish Queen Victoria each year. Take a dose twice each day . . .

61

MYRICK, *whispers*
   He's writing to the President?

ATKINSON, *whispering back*
   No, the Secretary of State.

MYRICK, *nodding, still puzzled*
   Oh.

CARNEGIE, *brandishing the bottle*
   For the Republican party I see nothing but disaster! Even
   Governor Roosevelt, with all his military glamour, would not
   carry New York State if the country were polled today. On
   the right platform, Bryan can beat us to death! I think he will
   drop free silver! Then look out!

SECOND SECRETARY *relieves him of the bottle.*

   Two doses a day — hot toddy at night. Take care of your
   health!

ATKINSON
   Bryan! Is he for us or against us?

MYRICK, *to* CARNEGIE
   I hope you have gotten hold of Mr. Bryan to correct his extraordinary error on the treaty.

ATKINSON
   How can he be *against* imperialism and *for* the treaty?

CARNEGIE
   He'll do the right thing in the end. I've written him another
   letter.

The BUTLER *appears, carrying luggage.*

BUTLER, *urgently*
Mr. Carnegie, sir, the newspaper men —

CARNEGIE, *good-naturedly*
Let the vultures in!

SECOND SECRETARY *jumps to help* CARNEGIE *into his jacket.*

MYRICK, *waving some literature*
I still haven't shown you our farm campaign —

CARNEGIE, *sweeping to the point*
How much do you need?

MYRICK
Ten thousand dollars?

CARNEGIE
I'll give you five. (*points him to the* CASHIER)

stentorian
Finally — (FIRST SECRETARY *lunges for his book*) — Madam
and I shall lunch with you in Washington with greatest pleas-
ure. Bitterly opposed to you, yet always your friend — Carnegie!

REPORTERS *burst into the room with* PHOTOGRAPHER. *The* MEN
smooth their hair, sober their faces. A picture is flashed.

REPORTERS
When are you leaving for Washington, Mr. Carnegie? What
will you say to the President? Will you meet with Senate
leaders? Do you have a plan to defeat the treaty?

CARNEGIE, *interrupting*
>Gentlemen: in what I am about to say, I am perfectly serious. I am not bluffing; I am not trifling. I am perfectly serious.

Deep silence. He reads a formal statement.

>Our leaders in Washington have eaten of the insane root of territorial expansion. We are in national delirium.

REPORTER, *coolly*
>Is there any truth to the rumor that your steel company is supplying arms to the Filipinos?

CARNEGIE, *out-cooling him*
>No, but I would be glad indeed to see them shoot back at us if we take them over by force.

REPORTER
>Mr. Carnegie, what would the Filipinos do if the United States pulls out?

CARNEGIE, *exasperated*
>What would they do? I don't suppose they'd chase us farther than San Francisco.

The REPORTERS *laugh nervously.* CARNEGIE *returns to his statement.*

>Therefore, I shall ask the President to send me to Manila, with authority to declare that the American government will recognize Philippine independence. I stand personally prepared to relieve the government of its obligation to the Spanish crown, and will offer to buy the Philippine Islands for twenty million dollars to set these people free . . .

The CASHIER *leaps up in protest.*

64

CASHIER
Twenty million? Mr. Carnegie!

Pandemonium. CARNEGIE'*s friends burst into delighted laughter.
The* REPORTERS *ask frantic questions.*

REPORTERS
Is this a joke? Wait for a picture! He must be crazy! Now
there's a man against imperialism! Puts his money where his
mouth is! Mr. Carnegie, what about the example of England?
Won't the Philippines be our India?

CARNEGIE *is preparing to leave. His* BUTLER *and* SECRETARIES
*help him on with coat and hat, hand him his umbrella. Looking
the perfect British gentleman, he pulls himself up sharply.*

CARNEGIE
India? India! Who said India? (*he is indignant*) My good
man, India is the curse of the British!

4
The United States Senate

"THE GREATEST QUESTION EVER DISCUSSED IN THIS CHAMBER"

SENATORS *are taking their seats. Among them are the Republicans supporting the treaty:* LODGE *of Massachusetts,*
FORAKER *of Ohio,* SPOONER *of Wisconsin; and Republicans
opposed to the treaty:* HOAR *of Massachusetts and* MASON
of Illinois. Democrats opposed to the treaty also appear:
TILLMAN *of South Carolina and* BACON *of Georgia.*

The PRESIDING OFFICER *gavels for order. The* CLERK *reads
the roll. Simultaneously, headlines.*

JANUARY, 1899
SENATE TAKES UP PEACE TREATY
STRONG OPPOSITION IS HINTED
Administration Alarmed
LODGE OF MASSACHUSETTS A LEADER OF FIGHT FOR RATIFICATION
HOAR OF MASSACHUSETTS BREAKS WITH ADMINISTRATION TO LEAD OPPOSITION
Eloquent Words of This Respected Senator Receive Closest Attention

GEORGE FRISBIE HOAR, "first among senators," is addressing the Senate. He is a man of seventy, with a mane of white hair and a cherubic, sometimes mischievous, expression.

HOAR

I dislike to differ from the President. I dislike to differ from so many of my party associates in this chamber, with whom I have for so many years trod the same path and sought the same goal. I am one of those men who believe that little that is great or good or permanent for a free people can be accomplished without the instrumentality of party. I have believed from my soul for half a century in the great doctrines and principles of the Republican party. I stood in a humble capacity by its cradle. I do not mean, if I can help it, to follow its hearse.

solemnly
Who can fail to read the signs of the times?

looks sharply at TILLMAN
Three states have adopted constitutions contrived to exclude Negroes from the right to vote. And now, with our great

66

problem unsolved, with ten millions of our own people — now thirty-five years after the Emancipation Proclamation — still waiting for the promise of their perfect freedom to be fulfilled, do you think you are asked to subject ten millions more to a government in which they have no voice?

Now, Mr. President. There are senators here (*catching* Spooner's *eye*) yet hesitating as to whether they will vote to ratify this treaty who will tell you privately that they loathe and hate this doctrine that we may acquire imperial powers or imperial regions by conquest.

I appeal to these gentlemen to answer to themselves the one great proposition: whether — even if that action be permitted by the letter of the Constitution — (*directed at* Foraker) — it be not repugnant to its form and spirit? Do you suppose it ever occurred to our forefathers that great rights were to be departed from whenever Congress should beguile itself by the specious pretense that it thought the thing it was doing was for the benefit of the victim?

And have not the Philippine people shown that they are fit for self-government? These are not savages. This is a people. They have a written constitution, a congress, courts, universities, newspapers, the Christian religion — and houses, works of art, pianos. They have statesmen who can debate questions of international law, and men who can organize governments. This is a nation, and it is a great crime to crush out its life.

Yet we are asked what else we can do with the Philippine Islands unless we are to sacrifice the immortal principles of the Declaration of Independence. Our imperialistic friends talk about "giving good government." Government is not a gift. It is a birthright. There can be no good government but self-government!

LODGE, *rising*
Will the Senator permit a question?

HOAR
Certainly.

LODGE
Does the Senator believe the capacity of a nation or a race for free and representative government to be a matter of guess-work? The form of government natural to the Asiatic — from Genghis Khan to an adventurer like Aguinaldo — has always been a despotism. You cannot change race tendencies in a moment. You cannot deal with an Asiatic as you can with an American or European.

HOAR
I wonder if the opposition can conceive that ideas of liberty are not related to the color of the skin? As soon as Spain was crushed, the Filipinos founded a republic — the first republic of the Orient.

LODGE
It does not follow because a government is called a republic that it is therefore a free government. They have no conception of free government! (*with a wry smile*) We must not confuse names with things.

Lights rise on a standing confrontation between JOHN SPOONER *of Wisconsin, an Administration man, and* "PITCHFORK BEN" TILLMAN *of South Carolina. Whenever* TILLMAN *speaks there is a moaning and a rustling among his colleagues.*

TILLMAN, *with a rasping drawl*
Now I ask the Senator from Wisconsin to withdraw any imputation upon the patriotism and good faith of the Philippine leader, Aguinaldo.

68

SPOONER, *astonished*

What I said did not even mention Aguinaldo! I merely said it would be the height of cruelty, the height of injustice to turn the Filipino people, whom we have just rescued from slavery to Spain, over into the hands of those irresponsible and trafficking leaders of theirs.

TILLMAN

There! And I understand the consent of the governed does not even enter into our ruling out there?

SPOONER, *wickedly*

Surely the Senator does not contend that the consent of the governed is wholly the ruling principle in South Carolina?

TILLMAN

We are discussing the Philippine Islands!

SPOONER

If the Senator from Aguinaldo will permit me to continue —

TILLMAN, *exploding*

Mr. President! I come not as a "senator from Aguinaldo," if you please —

SPOONER

I withdraw the remark.

TILLMAN

— but as a senator from Africa, if you please — South Carolina, with seven hundred fifty thousand colored population and only five hundred thousand whites.

TILLMAN *is on the subject of race: his colleagues settle down for the sideshow.*

Every man in this chamber, with few exceptions, who has had to do with the colored race plans to vote against the treaty, not because we are Democrats, but because we know what you are doing while you do not.

As though coming at the most opportune time possible, there just appeared in one of our magazines a poem by the greatest poet of England at this time — Mr. Rudyard Kipling — and it is called "The White Man's Burden." This man has lived in the Indies. He knows whereof he speaks.

waves a clipping of the poem
Now we of the South have borne this white man's burden of a colored race since Emancipation and before. We are not responsible for the presence among us of that people. We inherited our race problem. But you are going out in search of yours. You are undertaking to annex ten millions more of the colored race.

I want to remind you gentlemen from the North that your slogans about the brotherhood of man have gone glimmering down the ages. Has it come to this? Was the Civil War a mistake, then? And has the colored race no rights we are bound to respect at home or abroad?

Let me ask you then, if the Filipinos are not fit for self-government, how dared you put the southern states into the hands of Negroes, as being fit not only to govern themselves, but also to govern white men?

So we took the government away. We stuffed ballot boxes. We shot them. We are not ashamed of it. The Senator from Wisconsin would have done the same thing.

SPOONER, *protesting*
Mr. President!

TILLMAN, *enjoying it*
    I see it in his eye right now!

SPOONER
    Mr. President!

TILLMAN
    You don't love them any better than we do! "O ye hypocrites, ye hypocrites!"

SPOONER, *outraged*
    Mr. President!!

Other NORTHERNERS *leap to his defense.* HOAR *looks pained to have such an ally in the cause.* TILLMAN *grins.*

Lights up on WILLIAM MASON, *Illinois Republican and Senate freshman. An intense idealist, he is regarded as amusing, if somewhat inconsequential, by his colleagues.*

MASON
    We are told that the people of the Philippine Islands cannot govern themselves. No, no. They cannot govern themselves. I was told so the other day by a fellow Republican and beloved constituent who never governs himself fifteen minutes at a time back home in Illinois. But he was willing to take an assignment under the present Administration to govern all the Philippines at a fair salary.

Laughter

    But we are told we must civilize the Filipinos. I see that the great chief of that ethical society known as Tammany Hall has taken sides on this question. "Take the islands," says Mr. Croker, the Tammany chief. We can send him over there to teach municipal reform.

Laughter

Shall we send illustrated pictures showing the work of the mob in South Carolina?

TILLMAN
Mr. President, sir!

MASON
Can you deny it, sir?

scornfully
Where is the ambitious senator who wants to govern the Philippines? You do not speak their language. You do not know their schools. You cannot read their newspapers. Who wants to go, covered with the gewgaws and flubdubs of royalty, and have the natives keep the flies off your sacred person while you listen to the interpreter?

Laughter

Why do we promise liberty to Cuba, where we are pledged to remove our troops, and have another policy for the Philippines?

Ah yes, say my imperialistic friends, but we promised not to steal Cuba and we did not promise not to steal the Philippines!

FORAKER
Mr. President!

MASON
Like my distinguished colleague from Massachusetts I may be charged with speaking for rebels against the flag of my country.

looks at HOAR

I now take occasion to pay my tribute of honor and respect to that gentleman such as I bear toward few men in this life. Rebels? When did they take the oath of allegiance? Name the hour when they have not claimed the right of independence!

Some have been kind enough to say my seat was in danger. If I could turn the tide for the freedom of these people, I would give my seat as cheerfully as I would give a crust of bread . . .

5

Albany and Washington

TR and LODGE *are talking on the phone.*

TR
 Cabot?

LODGE
 Governor?

TR, *with* LODGE's *letter in hand*
 You seriously alarm me about the treaty!

LODGE
 It is the closest, hardest fight I have ever known in the Senate.

TR
 What an outrage on the country! They can't have *one third* of the Senate?

LODGE

On the surface they have more than one third. They could
defeat the treaty today if they could make them vote as they
talk.

TR

I don't believe it!

LODGE

But they have some very weak supporters. We may pull
through all right.

TR

Is there anything I can do? Would you like the New York
State Legislature to pass a resolution?

LODGE

Yes! We need all the outside help we can get.

relaxing

What a singular collection these anti-imperialists have gotten
together! Bryan and Carnegie and all the rest.

TR, *grimly*

All the lunatics . . . But your colleague, Senator Hoar!

LODGE

I wish Hoar hadn't associated himself with that crowd. You
appreciate the delicacy of my position there —

TR

I can't speak of him with moderation! He is little better than
a traitor! (*magnanimously*) I pardon him only on the ground
that he is senile.

74

6

The Senate Chamber

JOSEPH FORAKER of Ohio, *the precise legalist of the Republican side, is contending with* HOAR.

FORAKER

Mr. President, let me understand the Senator from Massachusetts.

turning to HOAR

What are we to think? Is it possible that this great and powerful nation of ours has no power to subserve its own necessary and constitutional purposes except only by the consent of the people who may for the time being be affected? The literal application of the Senator's doctrine would have turned back the *Mayflower* from our coast!

Suppose we acquire a coaling station that is situated upon an island in the sea. It is a constitutional purpose for which we acquire it.

Suppose it is essential for the safety of our interests there that we acquire the whole island, though there be a thousand, or one hundred thousand — as in the case of Hawaii — or a million people or more?

Suppose we acquire it for a purpose absolutely essential for the national defense? Would we jeopardize the national interests because somebody there had not been consulted? And suppose we consult the population and they object, or some of them object? What then?

75

MASON

If you want land, take Canada. That is nearer. Take Canada! They talk our language.

FORAKER

That is entirely different.

MASON

Oh yes, it is different. And I will tell you the difference. It is the difference between the British fleet and the fleet of Aguinaldo. That is all the difference!

FORAKER

That is nonsense.

MASON

Everything that does not suit the views of gentlemen who want to gobble up the Philippines is nonsense!

HOAR

If the Senator will allow me, I certainly affirm that if it were desirable, convenient, or we thought it essential for our national defense to annex outlying territory, and the people there possessing that territory objected, I should consider the claiming it, annexing it, subjecting it, under those circumstances, as a great national crime, to be repudiated, denounced; and I should consider that the United States had better go down beneath the waters of the Pacific in honor, rather than disgrace itself by doing that thing!

FORAKER

Now, Mr. President! Now we understand the Senator from Massachusetts!

HOAR

Yes, you understand me now. If we cannot live as a nation

without committing that crime, we ought to die as a nation without committing it. That is my doctrine.

FORAKER
I utterly repudiate that doctrine!

There is applause from the galleries. Several SENATORS *demand the floor.*

PRESIDING OFFICER
The gentleman from Georgia has the floor.

AUGUSTUS BACON, *Georgia Democrat and southern gentleman, is a respected figure in the Senate on questions of foreign policy.*

BACON
I shall occupy my colleagues' time but a moment. I wish merely to observe that there is no reason for the acquisition of the Philippine Islands that will not apply to the acquisition of other parts of Asia as well, each furnishing a reason why another part still beyond should be also acquired.

The logic of that policy will certainly require that we seek to bring under our dominion all countries whose people are too weak to resist our colossal power.

SPOONER
Oh!

BACON
Will our government abandon its peaceful career and become another Europe? I fear this reach-out for empire will lead to wars — not such a war with its trifling sacrifices through which we have just passed. But great wars, vast armies, ready on a day's notice to cope in bloody conflict with the military powers of the earth.

LODGE *and* FORAKER *jump up.*

LODGE
Mr. President!

FORAKER
The gentleman from Georgia —

BACON, *pleasantly, sitting*
I yield gladly to my colleague from Massachusetts.

LODGE
I have listened in amazement while specters of wrongdoing have been conjured up and charged as possible to the American people.

Mr. President, all this is so inconceivable to me that I cannot comprehend it!

FORAKER
That is right.

LODGE
There is no senator upon this floor who would not cut off his hand sooner than be false to the great traditions and ideals of American history. But I believe not merely in what the American people have done, but in what they are yet to do.

If we abandon those islands we leave them either to anarchy or to their seizure by some great Western power who will not uplift them and train them in the principles of freedom.

HOAR, *waspishly*
May I ask the Senator whether in protecting the people of the Philippine Islands from the ambition and cupidity of other nations, we are bound to protect them from our own?

LODGE, *snapping*

There are vast commercial and trade interests here. The world is no longer large enough to permit some of its more valuable portions to lie barren and ruined, the miserable result of foolish political experiments.

TILLMAN *growls in disgust.*

TILLMAN

The game here is simply to open the islands to capitalists and corporations who get in on the ground floor and map out their mines and such.

And the imperialists stand there and tell the American people they have gone into a partnership with God in this business, their motives are so holy and pure!

HOAR

Mr. President, if this is being a world power, I for one would rather be a world weakness.

Laughter

LODGE, *witheringly*

I cannot forecast the future as so many others have been able to do. I can but proceed step by step, and the only step I can see now to take is to ratify the treaty.

Would the opposition give the islands back to Spain?

HOAR

No, no.

MASON

The other side knows very well that is not what we ask.

Well then, let us look at it practically. We must either ratify the treaty or reject it, for I cannot suppose that anyone would seriously advance the proposition that the President be sent, hat in hand, to say to Spain, "I am here in obedience to the mandate of a minority of one third of the Senate to tell you that we have been too victorious and that you have yielded us too much and that I am very sorry I took the Philippines from you."

There is no magic in the word "minority." They have no monopoly of conscience or morals.

Suppose we reject the treaty. What follows? We hand the islands back to Spain — a thing to which I will never assent! — and continue the state of war. At the same time, we repudiate the President before the whole world, branding us in the eyes of civilized mankind as a people incapable of great affairs.

I want to get this country out of war and back to peace. I want to take the Philippines out of the hands of our war power, and give their inhabitants peace and self-government under the protective shield of the United States. I want to ratify the treaty, and then leave it to the American people, who have never failed in any great duty, to deal with those islands in that spirit of justice, humanity, and liberty which has made us all that we are today, or can ever hope to be.

Applause from the galleries

7
The White House

President McKinley is conferring with the aristocrat Hay, Secretary of State.

McKinley
Mr. Secretary, Andrew Carnegie was here. He is evidently serious about buying the Philippine Islands.

Hay roars with laughter.

Reporter
President McKinley meets almost daily with Secretary of State John Hay and Senate leaders. He has followed the Senate debate on the treaty with the closest attention.

McKinley, *distressed*
Carnegie says we'll be shooting down natives in thirty days.

Hay
Carnegie really seems to be off his head. He sends me Scotch whisky, and frantic letters signed, "Your bitterest opponent."

quoting Carnegie in high amusement
"The Administration will fall in irretrievable ruin the moment it shoots down one insurgent Filipino! The entire labor vote of America will be cast against us, and He will See that it is Done!"

McKinley, *sincerely puzzled*
Carnegie doesn't understand the situation at all. The Filipinos will welcome us as their best friends. And if we don't keep the Philippines, we'll be the laughing stock of the world.

LODGE *enters.*

MCKINLEY
Ah, Senator! What is the count?

LODGE
Mr. President, Hay, I am sorry to say that Heitfield went squarely over to the opposition today.

HAY
No!

MCKINLEY
How unfortunate.

LODGE
We had fifty-eight. Now we have fifty-seven. We need sixty. Still wavering are McEnery, McLaurin, and Jones of Nevada.

MCKINLEY, *anxiously*
What is your opinion?

LODGE
The result is doubtful. It is very trying, very disheartening.

HAY
It is preposterous! A treaty of peace, of *peace* mind you, ought to be ratified unanimously in twenty-four hours!

Headlines

DEMOCRATS IN ROW OVER TREATY

W. J. BRYAN URGES SENATE FOLLOWERS TO VOTE FOR RATIFICATION
His Intervention Dismays Treaty Opponents

VOTE SET IN TWO DAYS

82

8

The Senate Cloakroom

SENATORS *are scattered about in small groups. Two* REPORT-
ERS *are taking interviews. One is with Senator* WILLIAM
ALLEN *of Nebraska, Bryan's home state. Lingering nearby
is Senator* RICHARD PETTIGREW, *the South Dakota maverick
whose radical views offend everyone.*

ALLEN, *to* FIRST REPORTER
I look upon Mr. Bryan as a comet that has appeared in the
political heavens, that is seen upon the political horizon of
our country once in a generation only.

FIRST REPORTER
Senator Allen, why has Mr. Bryan —

ALLEN
Future generations will rank him as one of the greatest statesmen our country has produced.

FIRST REPORTER
But why —

ALLEN
And to assert, as the opposition does, that Mr. Bryan wants to
ratify the treaty to keep the issue of imperialism alive for use
against the President in the next campaign is contemptible and
scurrilous almost beyond imagination.

PETTIGREW *snorts derisively.*

FIRST REPORTER
Then why —

PETTIGREW

Bryan is not an able man. Able men do not go into politics. They stay in business and with the wealth they acquire through special privileges they support whichever of the two political parties will yield the largest net returns.

A SENATOR *turns around.*

SENATOR

Pettigrew, you're a damned radical!

PETTIGREW

I certainly hope so.

FIRST REPORTER

Bryan is opposed to imperialism, Senator Allen.

ALLEN

Irrevocably opposed.

FIRST REPORTER

Why then has he come out for the treaty?

ALLEN

The ratification of the treaty doesn't commit us to a colonial policy. It clears the way for recognition of the Philippine republic. And the Democrats can't take it on themselves to reject a peace treaty, you know.

PETTIGREW

I don't know which is worse, his political opportunism or his intellectual stupidity.

We can kill imperialism now, at once, by a vote of one third of the Senate.

After the treaty is ratified, any action by Congress for Philippine freedom will require a majority vote. Such a majority will be impossible to assemble because the Administration is having all the railroad and commercial interests, and every other interest that can be reached, put pressure on senators to sell out for any available favor, not excluding a cash consideration —

SENATORS *crowd around.* SECOND REPORTER *dashes over.*

SECOND REPORTER, *excited*
Senator Pettigrew, you believe some senators have accepted cash bribes to vote for ratification?

PETTIGREW
I charge the open purchase of votes right on the floor of the Senate!

A SENATOR *confronts* PETTIGREW.

SENATOR
Pettigrew, do not open that stinkpot before the press!

The REPORTERS *bolt with the story.*

PETTIGREW, *addressing his colleagues*
I say to you that if we annex the Philippines, the downfall of the Republic will date from that decision.

ALLEN
Calm down, Pettigrew. Suppose it's wrong to take the Philippines? Suppose we do make a blunder. Does anyone suppose that a single blunder, no matter how great, will wreck America? The proposition is ridiculous.

85

The group scatters. Two SENATORS *remain behind.*

FIRST SENATOR
    Pettigrew is a viper.

SECOND SENATOR
    He has a point about Bryan, though. I've always said Bryan
    would rather be wrong than be President.

They laugh.

*We hear the clicking of news tickers and the insistent ringing of
bells, indicating news of great importance. Headlines.*

FEBRUARY 5, 1899

TERRIBLE BATTLE AT MANILA

13,000 U.S. TROOPS ENGAGED

AWFUL SLAUGHTER

INSURGENTS TORN TO PIECES

NATIVES IN WILD PANIC

FILIPINO LOSS IS 4,000

40 AMERICANS DEAD

After the first few headlines, we hear the voice of a REPORTER.

REPORTER
    On the eve of the treaty vote in the Senate, serious fighting has
    broken out in Manila between American and Filipino insur-
    gent forces located there. Reports are that the Filipinos delib-
    erately opened fire on U.S. soldiers. President McKinley said
    tonight that the Manila engagement would, in his opinion,

86

insure the ratification of the treaty tomorrow. However, anti-imperialist senators are claiming victory . . .

Headlines

U.S. DENIES FILIPINO ARMISTICE REQUEST

ANOTHER BIG BATTLE EXPECTED NEAR MANILA

SENATE RATIFIES PEACE TREATY
WITH ONE VOTE TO SPARE

9

The Senate Chamber

A tumultuous exchange is in progress.

TILLMAN
A majority of this house was opposed to the treaty! But executive influence was brought to bear. The party whip was cracked —

turning on MASON
Men who thought the Filipinos ought to be left alone surrendered their independence — the treaty was ratified — and now the President has a legal excuse to prosecute a war!

MASON, *in agony*
I was willing to vote for the treaty because I was told it would stop the fighting. (*accusing* LODGE) I voted on the promise that afterwards we would pass a resolution and give these people a chance!

LODGE

The Filipinos deliberately precipitated an attack against a friendly nation —

TILLMAN

Friendly!

LODGE

What better proof of their unfitness for self-government than their senseless attack on us?

TILLMAN, *scoffing*

The reports all come from American sources.

MASON, *waving a newspaper at* **LODGE**

We are attacking people without arms who cannot defend themselves! Our troops go on shore and shell a town and seize it and burn it —

TILLMAN, *with macabre humor*

We shelled it, but *they* burned it, according to official reports. You must get your official information correct.

SPOONER

It is my own belief that the instigation of it all came from utterances made here on this floor. Let us not continue the mistake by sending messages of comfort to the enemies of our boys over there, fighting for life.

HOAR

Do not charge this thing upon us! The impudence! We have but proclaimed the doctrine of the Declaration of Independence!

Everyone speaks at once. **SPOONER** *raises his voice emotionally.*

SPOONER

I stand with the President! Our President asks, "Who will haul down the flag?"

HOAR

And who will haul down the President?

There is a sudden lull. BACON *speaks in troubled earnest.*

BACON

By what authority of the law can the President begin a war with the Filipinos? No declaration of war has been made by Congress. Mr. President, where are we drifting?

We are not charged with the duty of preserving order in Asia. Where are we drifting?

Silence. A moment of darkness.

"DESTINY IS NOT AS MANIFEST AS IT WAS LAST WEEK."
William Jennings Bryan

A solitary spotlight picks up ANDREW CARNEGIE.

CARNEGIE

One word from Mr. Bryan would have saved the country from disaster. There were seven staunch Bryan men anxious to vote against the treaty. I begged him to wire me that his friends could use their own judgment. But he was willing to sacrifice his country and his own personal convictions for party advantage. I could not be cordial to him for years afterward . . .

The White House

A military fanfare. An army color guard marches on with the flag. SOLDIERS *arrange themselves in stiff formation.* Mc-KINLEY *is about to sign the treaty. Behind him, the imperialists* LODGE, FORAKER, SPOONER.

McKINLEY

There are those who say we should not have taken the Philippine Islands without the consent of the people there. Did we need their consent to perform a great act for humanity? We were obeying a higher moral obligation, and did not require anybody's consent.

We are not a military people. We love peace. Peace brought us the Philippines, by treaty from Spain. Openly made was the treaty of peace. Openly ratified by the Senate of the United States, openly and publicly confirmed by the House of Representatives. Every step has been taken in obedience to the requirements of the Constitution. The President has no power, even if he were disposed — which he is not — to alienate a single foot of territory thus honestly acquired.

And now our flag waves in the Philippines. It waves not as the banner of imperialism; it waves not as the symbol of oppression. Wherever the flag goes, there go character, education, American intelligence, American civilization, and American liberty.

Now the men whom we emancipated from slavery say to the American government, "You can have peace if you will give us independence." Peace for independence, they say.

We never gave a bribe in all our history, and we will not now commence to do it. They assailed our sovereignty. And there will be no useless parley, no pause, until our flag shall float triumphantly in every island of that archipelago. We accept the responsibility at whatever cost it imposes. We will do our duty by them, as God gave us the light to see our duty, and with the approval of civilization.

In no other way, my friends, can we give peace to the national conscience, or peace to the world.

The band plays "Tramp, Tramp, Tramp, the Boys Are Marching." Carrying the American flag, the SOLDIERS *make the circuit of the stage, singing.*

SOLDIERS

> *Damn, damn, damn the Filipinos,*
> *Cross-eyed khakiak ladrones,*
> *Underneath the starry flag,*
> *Civilize 'em with a Krag,*
> *And return us to our own beloved homes!*

They march off, headed for the front.

11
Army Headquarters, Manila

"I COULD END THE WAR IN TWENTY DAYS . . ."

> Elwell S. Otis
> Commanding General
> Army VIII Corps
> Manila

Major General Otis strides up and down before maps and battleboards, dictating optimistic reports to the War Department.

Otis

Cable to War Department: Situation here rapidly improving. Insurgent army disintegrated and natives returning to villages displaying white flag.

Second Division under General MacArthur advancing north — now fifteen miles from Malolos, insurgent capital. Our loss thus far slight, enemy's heavy.

Aguinaldo charging Americans with initiative, calling all to resist "foreign invasion." Now he applies for cessation of hostilities and conference.

Have declined to answer.

If U.S. troops en route from San Francisco were now here, I could end the war in twenty days. — Otis, Army VIII Corps, Manila.

12

Press Tent, Behind the American Lines

Headlines

REBELS READY TO QUIT

THE BEGINNING OF THE END

ENEMY WILL MAKE LAST STAND AT MALOLOS

FIRST CORRESPONDENT
The Second Army Division, led by General Arthur MacArthur is sweeping northward today toward the rebel capital city of Malolos. General MacArthur is bent on the capture of the insurgent leader Aguinaldo, whose sway has already been broken by a series of defeats.

SECOND CORRESPONDENT
The soldiers at the front are discussing the chances of Aguinaldo's coming in to surrender tonight, or waiting until tomorrow morning, when General MacArthur may reach the capital city.

13
The War Department, Washington

REPORTER
Washington, March 29. The War Department.

turning to SPOKESMAN
Do you believe the fighting will end tomorrow, when General MacArthur takes Malolos?

WAR DEPARTMENT SPOKESMAN, *beaming*
The insurgents are fighting with great desperation. This is an indication that they have staked everything on the outcome of this fight for their capital city. When they lose, we believe Aguinaldo will submit rather than prolong a hopeless struggle.

MacArthur's Lines at Malolos

Headlines

MALOLOS IS OURS!

MacARTHUR'S GREAT VICTORY!

AGUINALDO'S POWER FALLS WITH LOSS OF MALOLOS

END OF WAR AT HAND

SOLDIERS *cheer, laugh, and fire shots in the air. In a holiday mood, they toss about a crude effigy of Aguinaldo on the tip of a bayonet.*

SOLDIERS, *singing*
>Aguinaldo leads a sloppy life.
>He eats potatoes with a knife.
>Once a year he takes a scrub
>And leaves the dirt inside the tub.

15

The Press Tent

CORRESPONDENT

General MacArthur's troops occupied the rebel capital of Malolos at 9:30 this morning. The Americans found the town in flames, set on fire by the enemy, and deserted. The main force of the insurgents, together with the inhabitants, had left the capital two days before. Apparently, the fall of Malolos is not of great significance to the insurgents.

16

The War Department

REPORTER

Washington, March 31. The news from Manila today is a grievous disappointment to the War Department and to the President. Isn't it true, sir, that the Administration counted upon a decisive battle at Malolos, and a decisive defeat there of the forces under Aguinaldo?

WAR DEPARTMENT SPOKESMAN

Not necessarily. General Otis is about to execute another important movement, and little further resistance is expected. Regrettably, the time for peaceable negotiations simply has not come.

17

Army Headquarters, Manila

"IMPORTANT RESULTS WITHIN THREE WEEKS . . ."

> Elwell S. Otis
> Commanding General
> Army VIII Corps
> Manila

OTIS, *dictating a cable, cheerful as always*

Last night, about one thousand insurgent troops gained access to Manila behind our lines and made determined effort to burn city.

The enemy was completely routed. His loss, five hundred killed, American loss slight. Manila now quiet. Natives respectful and cheerful.

We are preparing for a continued active campaign, and important results will be accomplished within three weeks — Otis, Army VIII Corps, Manila.

18

In the Field, Luzon

FIRST CORRESPONDENT
April 14, 1899. "Just watch our smoke!" That is the motto the Minnesota and Oregon regiments have adopted since their experiences of the last few days.

Near the town of Titatia, an American boy was found shot, his stomach cut open. Immediately orders were received to burn the town. Hundreds of natives were reportedly killed.

SECOND CORRESPONDENT *appears with two American* SOLDIERS.

FIRST SOLDIER
The word was passed down the line to take no prisoners. We picked them off like jackrabbits.

SECOND SOLDIER
I don't know how many niggers the Tennessee boys did kill. They wouldn't take any prisoners. One company of 'em was sent into headquarters with thirty prisoners. They got there with a hundred chickens.

SECOND CORRESPONDENT
What did they do with the prisoners?

SECOND SOLDIER *shrugs.*

The light grows red and intense. The crackling of thatch is heard. Behind the cool professionalism of the CORRESPONDENTS' *voices, we hear the muted sounds of human distress — women shrieking, babies wailing — and cries of frightened livestock.* SOLDIERS *appear, disappear, reappear. They are burning the countryside.*

FIRST CORRESPONDENT
On the nineteenth, General Wheaton made up his mind to teach the insurgents and the people of the country generally that whenever they attacked our lines or lured us into a trap, we would hit back again very hard.

SECOND CORRESPONDENT
The Twenty-second Infantry started at daylight, driving the rebels before them and setting the torch to everything burnable in their course. Their trail was eight miles long and the smoke of burning buildings and rice heaps obscured the landscape for many hours.

THIRD CORRESPONDENT
North of Manila, practically the entire region for thirty miles, once filled with dozens of pretty towns and villages, each with its interesting Spanish church building, has been gutted by fire. Every hut is a heap of ashes. It is a desolate picture. Nearly all the people have fled. The roads are strewn with furniture and clothing. One sees only a few forlorn and wary noncombatants.

SECOND CORRESPONDENT
Mr. F. A. Blake of the American Red Cross described the effect

of the American advance to the *New York Times* correspondent in Manila . . .

BLAKE

I never saw such execution in my life. I saw arms and legs
nearly demolished, total decapitation, horrible wounds in
chests and abdomens. I counted seventy-nine dead natives in
one small field, and learned that on the other side of the river
their bodies were actually stacked up for breastworks.

One thing I can tell you. This rush is putting the fear of God
in the natives.

19
Army Headquarters, Manila

"IMPROVED CONDITIONS WITHIN ONE MONTH . . ."

> Elwell S. Otis
> Commanding General
> Army VIII Corps
> Manila

OTIS, *to* CORRESPONDENTS, *impressively*

The fighting qualities of the American troops have been a revelation to all inhabitants. The insurgent army is defeated, shat-
tered, and discouraged. Signs of their weakness are more ap-
parent daily. All armed opposition will cease when the Luzon
rebels are overpowered.

FIRST CORRESPONDENT

When do you think that will be, sir?

OTIS

I hope to report greatly improved conditions within a month.

SECOND CORRESPONDENT
   You do not anticipate difficulty on the other islands?

OTIS
   Oh no! The news from the Visayan Islands is more encouraging every day.

   briefs the CORRESPONDENTS, *using a map pointer*
   Reports from Panay indicate improvement.

   Reports from Negros are most encouraging. Inhabitants there are enthusiastic for American supremacy.

   Cebu is quiet.

   The inhabitants of Samar and Leyte have asked for United States troops, and these islands have been occupied.

   Remember this. The better class of people here are anxious for peace and stable government. I'm encouraged to hope for great improvement.

Headlines

PHILIPPINE REBELLION SPREADS

BAD SITUATION AT NEGROS
Otis Hurries Troops There

UPRISING IN SAMAR

OUTBREAK ON LEYTE

FIGHTING ON ILOILO

**AGUINALDO'S POWER EXTENDS
FAR BEYOND LUZON**

The War Department

FIRST REPORTER, *gravely*
The War Department announced today that the total number of casualties on the American side in the first six weeks of hostilities was 1,021.

The inadequacy of the American forces is said to be responsible for the large total loss in a number of small encounters. The insurgents are now reoccupying towns Americans have had to abandon, simply for want of men to hold them.

SECOND REPORTER *appears with General* SHAFTER, *an old war hero, now in mothballs. He is in uniform, sagging with medals.*

SECOND REPORTER
General Shafter, from your experience in fighting the Indians out west, what would your plan be for ending the fighting in the Philippines?

SHAFTER, *importantly*
My plan would be to disarm the natives of the Philippine Islands, even if we have to kill half of them to do it. Then I would treat the rest of them with perfect justice.

The White House

FIRST REPORTER, *to White House* SPOKESMAN
Is it true that the President has called a special cabinet meeting this morning to consider recommendations of additional troops in the Philippines?

SPOKESMAN, *authoritatively unresponsive*
The President is confident of General Otis' ability to subjugate the enemy with the thirty thousand troops now in the field.

FIRST REPORTER
Then —

SPOKESMAN
There is no intention at present of increasing the forces in the Philippines.

SECOND REPORTER
Nevertheless, it is privately conceded in Washington that great reinforcements are needed. It is believed that at least fifty thousand soldiers will be required, and experienced officers are saying that many more than fifty thousand are needed for complete American control of the islands.

22

Army Headquarters, Manila

OTIS *is being interviewed by* CORRESPONDENTS.

FIRST CORRESPONDENT
General are you familiar wih this pamphlet, *Cost of a National Crime?* Mr. Edward Atkinson of the so-called Anti-Imperialist League is sending these to American officers and men here.

OTIS, *stiffly*
These are being taken from the mails and destroyed by order of the War Department.

FIRST CORRESPONDENT
Have you read the pamphlet?

OTIS
Unfortunately, great encouragement is being given to Aguinaldo by some of our public men who are opposing the President's policy.

SECOND CORRESPONDENT
Do you think they should be silenced?

OTIS
Let me say that some of our worst enemies are those of our own household.

THIRD CORRESPONDENT
Sir, the Associated Press reports that Aguinaldo has again asked for an armistice as a condition to precede negotiations.

OTIS, *snappishly*
I have denied the request. Negotiations with the insurgents
cost our soldiers' lives and prolong our difficulties. However,
we have reason to believe that the populous province of Cavite
will surrender in a few days. This of course will break the
power of the insurrection in Luzon.

23

The War Department

WAR DEPARTMENT SPOKESMAN, *to* REPORTER
Certainly the boys will be home by Christmas. Our plans con-
template the subjugation of the insurrection before the opening of the rainy season.

REPORTER
That's excellent news, sir.

SPOKESMAN
Yes, we're very pleased.

A roll of thunder. We hear the downpour of a tropical rainstorm.

24

Manila

OTIS *alone, wearing a poncho, drenched, miserable*

OTIS, *after a long pause*
Rainy season . . . unparalleled heavy rainfall . . . extreme

heat . . . bad roads . . . severe typhoons . . . sickness increased. Troops worked to limit of endurance.

However, nothing alarming.

blows his nose unhappily
The insurgents state that if attempt at so-called forcible domination continues, they will prolong the war . . . indefinitely . . .

Sounds of rainfall continue. Headlines.

REBELS EXTEND GUERRILLA WARFARE

NEW DANGER OF JUNGLE AMBUSHES

TEN ADDITIONAL REGIMENTS
ORDERED TO MANILA

A LONG WAR IS PREDICTED

25

An Army Barracks

A group of American SOLDIERS, *unshaven, ill-fed. They are at rest, writing letters, playing cards, thinking. One strums a mandolin. The sound of rainfall is intense. A young* VOLUNTEER *is writing home.*

VOLUNTEER
The heat was something horrible. Our heads were splitting. I drank water from pools green with slime. That's all that saved us that day. Men marched until they fell down and fainted by the side of the column. I saw one man in convul-

sions. Then the sky just opened up and tried to drown us out . . . We had nothing to eat, and nothing to sleep on, not even a poncho . . . Next day we marched waist-deep in sloughs of running water and all the natives who were fighting us the day before came out from the houses with white flags and bowed and scraped . . .

Enlisted men are playing poker. A battle-tough SERGEANT, *veteran from the Cuban campaign, speaks as he deals.*

SERGEANT

So we were bringing our prisoners out of the brush when this little brownie nigger with his leg broken and half his face shot away comes splashing along the rice ditch like a water dog. He sees us, drops his gun and yells, "Amigo, mucho amigo."

The men greet this ironically. They know about "amigos."

That boy was a sight to look at. The blood was coming from him like out of a spigot. The captain wrapped his own first-aid bandage around the little worm — he was no bigger than a tin cup — and the boy kisses his hand, respectful-like, like a dog.

Mild hilarity. One soldier does an imitation of a dog, another does a whining spiel in mock Spanish-Tagalog. They subside, studying their cards as the SERGEANT *finishes the story.*

Then the captain and Steve Waters carried the little boy to a shack we passed a couple of hundred yards back. They was going to get the hospital men. They wasn't gone two minutes and I begun to get uneasy. So I took a couple of men with me and pushed back to the shack. There on the floor was the captain, and Waters lay across him.

The others mutter, "Goddamn," "Christ."

Some of the niggers carved them up. The little amigo was gone.

SOLDIER, *angry, nearly crying*
Damn! I am in my glory when I can sight my gun on some dark skin and pull the trigger! Damn!!

A JUNIOR OFFICER, *drinking at a table, turns to the* SERGEANT.

JUNIOR OFFICER
Look, there's no use mincing words about it. We can't have it both ways. We have to conquer and hold the islands or get out. The question is, which is it going to be? If we decide to stay, we have to bury all these qualms and scruples and *stay*. Look: we exterminated the American Indians and I guess most of us are proud of it, or at least we believe the end justified the means. And we're going to have to do the same thing with this other race standing in the way of progress if it is necessary. At least that's what I think — either finish the job or get out.

Quiet. The sound of rainfall and a mournful mandolin. The MANDOLIN PLAYER *half sings, half hums, softly.*

YOUNG SOLDIER
I didn't like to fire. The little brown beggars were so plucky and exposed themselves so bravely. There were women there shot down cooking for their husbands and brothers. There were lads of twelve and fourteen firing bravely to the last, and old men who could hardly see . . . I am not afraid — and I am always ready to do my duty — but I would like someone to tell me, what are we fighting for?

It rains harder. The YOUNG SOLDIER *is caught in his private world of doubt.*

26

A Chicago Meeting Hall

Above the podium hangs a bright banner.

> # REPUBLIC OR EMPIRE?
> ### ANTI-IMPERIALIST LEAGUE
> ### NATIONAL CONGRESS

CARL SCHURZ *is speaking in moral outrage.*

SCHURZ

And now that the imperialists have got the country into this frightful mess, what have they to propose? What is their answer? More soldiers! Seventy thousand of them now! More guns! More blood! More devastation! Kill! Kill! Kill! And when we have killed enough, so that further resistance stops, then we shall see. Translated from smooth phrase into plain English, that is their program.

Two years ago, the prediction of such a possibility would have been regarded as a hideous nightmare, as the offspring of a diseased imagination. But today, we are engaged in a wanton, wicked, and abominable war. So it is called by thousands of American citizens, and so it is felt to be, I have no doubt, by an immense majority of the American people. It is cursed by many of our very soldiers whom our government orders to shoot down innocent people. And who will deny that this war could have been avoided?

Prolonged applause and chanting: "Bring the boys home . . . Bring the boys home . . ." Headlines.

10,000 HEAR CARL SCHURZ DENOUNCE WAR IN CHICAGO

PROTEST MEETINGS IN MANY OTHER CITIES

EX-PRESIDENTS CLEVELAND AND HARRISON SUPPORT ANTI-IMPERIALISTS
Movement Attracts Many University Presidents, Professors, Former Government Officials

THIRD PARTY ANTI-IMPERIALIST TICKET HINTED

SCHURZ
   President McKinley —

There is booing and hissing.

   The President —

More booing

I could hardly believe my eyes when I read in a recent speech by the President this amazing statement: "To the party of Lincoln has come another supreme opportunity, which it has bravely met, in the liberation of ten millions of the human race from the yoke of imperialism." The party of Lincoln! Liberation!

Laughter

There is poetic genius in this sentence!

Here is another example of the President's candor. He says that the war was begun by the insurgents. "An attack evidently prepared in advance," he says, "was made all along the American lines."

Everybody knows that our men actually began the slaughter, that the role of the insurgents was strictly defensive. That General Otis —

Scattered boos

— refused to stop the bloodshed when Aguinaldo sued for a cease-fire.

The President says that if we withdraw our forces from the Philippines, the Filipinos would at once drop into anarchy, and cut one another's throats. It sounds like a ghastly jest that in nine months we should have killed thirty thousand of those people for the purpose of preventing them from killing each other. No "anarchy" in the Philippines would shed half as much blood as we have already shed.

furiously

In my whole long life I have never known of such systematic use of distortion of history, hypocritical cant, garbling of documents, and false pretense. It is the hugest confidence game ever practiced upon a free people, sustained by the machinery of deception of our present war censorship — which is practiced not only in Manila but directly by the Administration in Washington. This is a war not merely against the Filipinos, but against ourselves as a free people!

Applause

There are few Americans who do not frankly admit their regret that this war should ever have happened. It is not merely the bungling conduct of military operations but a serious trouble of conscience that disturbs the American heart about this war, and this trouble of conscience will not be allayed by a more successful military campaign, just as fifty years ago the trouble of conscience about slavery could not be allayed by any compromise. Yet many people now, as the slavery compromisers did then, try to ease their minds by saying, "Well, we are in it, and now we must do the best we can."

Have you considered what this means?

glares at his audience
Imagine a future President to be no model of public virtue and wisdom, but a man of uncontrollable combativeness of temperament; or a man of extreme partisan spirit, who honestly believes the victory of his party to be necessary for the salvation of the universe. Imagine such a future President plunging the country into war-like conflicts of his own motion, with only some legal technicalities to cover his usurpation. And imagine that however bad a mess he may have got the country into he may count upon the people to cry down everybody who opposes it because "we are in it"!

Can you conceive a more baneful precedent to the peace and security of the country than the precedent we establish by acquiescing to this policy?

Cries of "That is right!"

What is to be done? Precisely because "we are in it," let us turn out of power those who got us into it, and put into power men who wish to get us out of it! At this congress I have met men from thirty states. All of them voted for McKinley. Not one of them is going to do so again!

Great applause

Now if a cruel fate should force me to choose between Republican McKinley and the imperialistic policy, and Democrat Bryan —

110

Cries of "No!"

—as the anti-imperialist candidate, I should consider it my duty—

Cries of "No! No!"

—to swallow my personal disgust and try to defeat imperialism at any cost. But there is a very widespread feeling that the people have permitted themselves long enough, and too long, to be forced by two rotten old party carcasses to choose between evils. I ask you to consider whether it will not be our best policy to strike out boldly for a new party . . .

He is drowned out by applause.

27

A Smoke-filled Room

Solemn funeral music. Three political Bosses *appear, dressed in high mourning, top hats held respectfully across their chests, cigars stoking from their mouths. Headlines.*

VICE-PRESIDENT GARRETT HOBART IS DEAD
Nation Mourns Loss

The Bosses *are introduced to the audience by a* Reporter.

Reporter
United States Senator Thomas Collier Platt, Republican leader of the state of New York.

United States Senator Matthew Quay, Republican leader of the state of Pennsylvania.

United States Senator Marcus Alonzo Hanna, Chairman of the Republican National Committee.

The Bosses *relax abruptly and fall to intense discussion around a table holding whisky and glasses.*

PLATT, *to* HANNA, *warily*
Senator, the Party needs strength in the West, and the Party needs strength in the East. Now how can we accomplish that in the person of one vice-presidential candidate?

HANNA, *making a joke*
We'll nominate a western banker.

QUAY, *cagey*
How about an eastern cowboy?

PLATT
Roosevelt is the man. Governor of New York. A Rough Rider. They love him out west. In his western trip they cheered him at every stop just as if he was running for President.

HANNA, *suspiciously*
Maybe he is.

PLATT
Can you doubt his loyalty to McKinley? The President's Philippine policy doesn't have a stronger backer in the country.

They laugh. ROOSEVELT's *support may be too strong.*

HANNA, *warily*

Roosevelt is a valuable man, Senator. The question is: where is he most valuable? If we run him for Vice-President, who will win your election for you in New York?

PLATT

I appreciate your interest in our state problems, Senator, but I very much doubt the New York delegation can be prevented from putting Roosevelt's name in nomination at the convention.

HANNA

I know it is hard to control enthusiasm for favorite sons, but we are all bound to respect the President's wishes. If Mr. McKinley does not want Governor Roosevelt's name put in nomination, then I cannot believe the New York delegation would do so.

QUAY, *taking a huge puff on his cigar*
Now let's simplify this thing.

to PLATT

What you mean to say, Platt, is that you want to force Hanna here to take Theodore because the big insurance companies and the great corporations and all the big-moneyed men of New York want Theodore *out*.

to HANNA

And you, Hanna, you don't want Theodore, you don't like him, you don't trust him, you can't control him, and since you are the President's chief advisor in political matters, and since you control the convention, you think that settles it.

PLATT *and* HANNA *puff their cigars in silent fury.*

Now there is a question in my mind you haven't touched on. Will Theodore accept the nomination if it is offered to him?

The others shrug this off: of course he'll accept.

I don't know. The vice-presidency is a monastic office. It is an office from which no man since Martin Van Buren has been elected to the White House. On the contrary, it is an office from which men have been wont to retire to abandoned farms. Roosevelt is an active man. Why would he want to become a political corpse?

HANNA *nods, pleased that* QUAY *is an ally.*

On the other hand. I know Theodore well. If you can get enough people hollering for him to take the job — common people, mind you, not nice people — he'll insist on being Vice-President.

PLATT *nods.* QUAY *now openly advises him.*

Just tell Theodore that the people need him in Washington and then start people out west writing to him to take it. I've known Theodore a long time.

Finally HANNA *understands. This is not a meeting: it's a conspiracy.*

HANNA, *jumping up*
Whose side are you on, Matt Quay?

QUAY, *rising*
I bear you no personal ill will, Hanna. But it was a great disappointment to my loyal Pennsylvania friends that the propriety of my holding a seat in the Senate was publicly questioned this session . . .

114

PLATT, *rising*

Hanna, face the music. You can no more prevent Roosevelt's nomination than you can stop Niagara Falls.

HANNA

Not over my blazing damned dead body you won't! Don't you two realize that if Roosevelt is nominated there will be just one life between that crazy man and the presidency of the United States?!

QUAY, *picking up his whisky glass*

Gentlemen: I give you Theodore Roosevelt, the next Vice-President of the United States. Let us tremble while we drink.

They drink, with as many conflicting emotions as ever led man to drink.

28

A Hotel Room at the Republican National Convention

Music and activity from the convention floor drift into ROOSEVELT's *hotel room, where he is dressing in an agitated state.* LODGE *is worried.*

TR

I won't do it! I'm not going to do it!

Look here, old man. Now Platt tells me that if I don't accept second place on the ticket, he'll block my renomination for governor. That makes it impossible for me to run for Vice-President! I've made up my mind. If there's going to be war

with the machine, there's going to be war! We'll see who's
stronger, Platt or I.

LODGE
Hurrah! But if you step down there they will nominate you
and nothing can stop it. The western men demand it. They
feel you strengthen the ticket.

TR
They regard me as a fellow barbarian, that's all.

LODGE
You simply don't grasp your hold on the voters!

TR, *the truth comes out*
I'd rather be anything than Vice-President.

LODGE, *pleading*
Think of your interests.

TR
I am. I want a job with work in it. Secretary of War —

LODGE, *exasperated*
Elihu Root is Secretary of War.

TR
Maybe we could get Root the vice-presidential nomination?

LODGE
Theodore!

TR
I'd like to be in the Senate . . .

116

LODGE
There are no openings in New York.

TR
I would *love* to be first civil governor of the Philippine Islands!

Sounds from the convention grow louder.

LODGE
We must leave.

TR
If the vice-presidency could lead to the Philippine job then the question would be entirely altered. But there would be a strong feeling — altogether unreasonable — against my resigning as Vice-President to take another post. I don't know why — the succession is arranged in the Secretary of State —

LODGE
Theodore! For heaven's sake!

TR
If they nominate me it will be impossible to get it out of the heads of a number of people that the machine had forced me into it for their own sinister purposes and that I had yielded from weakness.

LODGE, *resigned*
All right. Go down there and refuse it.

TR
I didn't say I would not *under any circumstances* accept the nomination . . .

LODGE, *relief showing in a trace of a smile*
Let us leave. We are late.

TR, *grumbling*
But I would rather be anything than Vice-President! I would
rather be a professor of history than Vice-President!

LODGE
My God!

In a sour mood, TR *plunks a Rough Rider hat on his head, and
walks out to a roar of adulation.* DELEGATES *surround him.*

29
The Conventions

*Banners, bunting, balloons, posters, placards, funny hats
with names of states — the political conventions. A band
plays a medley of patriotic tunes. Headlines.*

JULY 5, 1900

DEMOCRATS NOMINATE BRYAN

ADLAI STEVENSON OF ILLINOIS
TAKES SECOND PLACE

BRYAN CALLS IMPERIALISM THE
"PARAMOUNT ISSUE"
Also Attacks Monopolies and Trusts

Failure to Drop Issue of Free Silver
May Hurt Campaign

We hear a fragment of a nominating speech.

We call him "Teddy." "Teddy" was the child of Fifth Avenue. He was the child of the clubs. He was the child of the exclusiveness of Harvard College. He went west and became a cowboy. And the cowboy became a soldier, and the soldier became a hero, rushing up a hill, pistol in hand, shouting, "Give them hell, boys! Give them hell!"

Headlines

McKINLEY BY ACCLAMATION

REPUBLICANS STAND ON NATIONAL PROSPERITY
"Full Dinner Pail" Is Theme of Campaign

ROOSEVELT TAKES CONVENTION BY STORM
Says Bryan Would Bring Disaster at Home,
Cowardice Abroad

Launches Whirlwind Tour Across the Country

Thunderous ovation from the floor. The band plays Teddy's tune — "There'll Be a Hot Time in the Old Town Tonight." ROOSEVELT appears, waving from the platform of a train.

TR, *to the audience, as the train slides from view*
The thing could not be helped. It was simply impossible to resist so spontaneous a feeling.

30
Mr. Dooley Follows the Campaign

The Archey Road saloon. MR. DOOLEY is indulging in a beer with MR. HENNESSEY.

Mr. Dooley

Well, sir, if they'se anny wan r-runnin' in this campaign but me frind Tiddy Rosenfelt, I'd like to know who it is.

It ain't Mack. It ain't Bryan. It ain't Adly. 'Tis Tiddy alone that's r-runnin', an' he ain't r-runnin', he's gallopin'.

South Dakota turned out as wan man an' exchanged shots iv greetin' with him. It was shutters up at th' joolry store an' glass out at th' saloon.

An' whin Thaydore kisses a baby, Hinnissy, thousands iv mothers in all corners iv th' land hear th' report, an' th' baby knows it's been kissed, an' bears th' hon'rable scars through life. Twinty years fr'm now, th' counthry will be full iv young fellows lookin' as tho' they'd gradyated fr'm a German college.

In this way he proves that 'tis by illicitin' himself, an' th' other la-ad on th' ticket, that free silver, arnychy, vilence, and anti-imperyalism can be cr-rushed.

Mr. Hennessey

Yes, but otherwise, 'tis a dead campaign.

Mr. Dooley

'Twill liven up, I begin to see the signs. A dillygation iv Mormons has started fr'm Dimmycratic headquarthers with instructions to thank th' Prisident f'r his manly stand in favor iv poly-gamy, an' th' Raypublican comity has undher consideration a letter fr'm long-term criminals advisin' their collagues at large to vote f'r Willum Jennings Bryan, th' frind iv crime.

Mr. Hennessey

Ye don't say.

MR. DOOLEY

I do. Mark Hanna rings f'r his sicrety an' asks, "Where is th' secret communication fr'm Bryan found on an arnychist at Patherson, New Jersey, askin' him to blow up th' White House?"

"It's in th' hands iv th' type-writer," says th' sicrety.

"Thin call up an emplymint agency," says Hanna, "an' have a dillygation iv Jesuites dhrop in on Bryan with a message fr'm th' Pope proposin' to bur-rn all Protestant churches th' night befure illiction." 'Twill liven up.

shakes his head
'Tis a quare campaign, Hinnissy. No wan is goin' to vote th' way he believes.

MR. HENNESSEY

How ar're ye goin' to vote ye'ersilf?

MR. DOOLEY

I dinnaw. Sure they ought to have wan place f'r a citizen to vote f'r his principles, an' another to vote f'r his candydate.

31
A New York Pier

An expectant crowd holds up signs, "Welcome home, Mark Twain!" REPORTERS crowd about the great man as he steps off the gangplank.

FIRST REPORTER

Welcome home, Mr. Twain. Good to have you back in America.

TWAIN

After nine years, it's good to be back.

SECOND REPORTER

Have you been following the election, Mr. Twain? Are you for the President?

TWAIN

As near as I can find out, I'm an anti-imperialist. I used to be a red-hot imperialist. I wanted the American eagle to go screaming into the Pacific. But no more.

FIRST REPORTER

You are going to vote for Mr. Bryan, then?

TWAIN

Not after he backed that treaty.

SECOND REPORTER

You mean you won't vote?

TWAIN

Oh I wish I'd been here two months ago. I'd have gone on the stump against both candidates. If there was another party, even an Anti-Doughnut Party, neither fellow would get elected.

32
Behind the Scenes

Senator PETTIGREW *has a chat with the audience.*

PETTIGREW

Historically, the two parties represent varying points of view as to the best method of robbing the workers. The Democrats used to favor slavery as a method, but those differences were ironed out during the Civil War.

Now we anti-imperialists agreed that it was foolish to depend on either of the two political parties to get us out of the Philippines, as both parties were simply the servants of the great corporations which wanted to exploit the islands.

We had a conference at the Plaza Hotel in New York, where we decided to start a third party and to organize it in every county in the United States. About eighteen of us were there, including Andrew Carnegie. I was the only United States senator.

Carnegie said he would give as much money, dollar for dollar, as all the rest of us could raise toward the campaign. He subscribed $25,000 on the spot as a pledge of good faith, and wrote out a check for fifteen.

Next thing I heard, Carnegie refused to pay another penny for the third party. He even refused to see me to talk about it. So I went down to Wall Street and asked some friends what had happened to Carnegie. This is what I heard.

Just at this time, the formation of the steel trust was planned by the great capitalistic combinations of the country. They were organizing a corporation with a billion dollars' worth of stock. This is the corporation that became U.S. Steel. The steel people, of course, heard that Carnegie was involved in the third party. They served notice on him that if Carnegie insisted on pursuing it, they would drop the trust.

Carnegie abandoned the whole third party movement and went in for the election of McKinley. Subsequently Carnegie received his hundreds of millions from the steel trust, retired from active business, and began to build monuments to himself all over the world.

The third party movement collapsed, and most of the anti-imperialists went for Bryan.

My colleague George Hoar of course went for McKinley. He said he couldn't forgive Bryan about the treaty, but the fact is, the worthy Massachusetts statesman went to dinner when the dinner bell rang. It was not that he cared so much for the actual meal, but it came hard to him to see his old table-mates in the Party sitting without him.

I supported Bryan. He was the last of the Democratic leaders to make a stand against the vested interests. He was not corrupt. But he was weak, vacillating, uncertain, ignorant of the forces shaping American life, a maker of phrases as a substitute for thought (*he shrugs*) — an American politician.

Sounds of inebriate celebration at Republican Headquarters. Headlines.

33
Mr. Dooley Wraps up the Election

The Archey Road saloon. MR. DOOLEY *and* MR. HENNESSEY
are studying the election returns.

MR. HENNESSEY
I see that Tiddy —

MR. DOOLEY
Don't be disrayspictful! He's Vice-Prisidint now.

MR. HENNESSEY
I don't believe it.

MR. DOOLEY
It's sthrange about th' vice-prisidincy. It isn't a crime exactly.
Ye can't be sint to jail f'r it. But it's a kind iv a disgrace.

It is princip'lly, Hinnissy, because iv th' Vice-Prisidint, that
most iv our prisidints have enjoyed such rugged health. "D'
ye know," says th' Prisidint to th' Vice-Prisidint, "ivry time I
see you I feel tin years younger?" (*thumping his newspaper*)
But didn't we give it to 'em, Hinnissy?

MR. HENNESSEY
To who?

MR. DOOLEY
Why, to th' Dimmycrats iv course.

MR. HENNESSEY
Ye're a Dimmycrat ye'ersilf!

MR. DOOLEY, *incensed*
Not me! I'm the hottest kind of Raypublican.

MR. HENNESSEY
But th' Dimmycrats ar-re r-right.

MR. DOOLEY
They're always r-right. 'Tis their position. Th' Dimmycrats ar-re r-right, an' th' Raypublicans has th' jobs.

MR. HENNESSEY, *sighing*
I wondher if us Dimmycrats will iver ilict a prisidint again.

MR. DOOLEY, *dismissing the concern*
Man an' boy, I've seen th' Dimmycratic Party hangin' to th' ropes a score iv times. I've seen it dead and burrid and th' Raypublicans kindly buildin' a monymint f'r it. I've gone to sleep nights wondhring where I'd throw away me vote afther this, an' whin I woke up, there was that crazy-headed ol' loon iv a party, with its hair sthreamin' in its eyes, an' an axe in its hand, chasin' Raypublicans into th' tall grass.

Somethin' will turn up, ye bet, Hinnissy. Th' Raypublican Party may die iv overfeedin'. An annyhow, they'se always wan ray iv light ahead. We're sure to have hard times.

MR. HENNESSEY *is morose. Long silence.* MR. DOOLEY *goes through the paper.*

MR. HENNESSEY, *listlessly*
What's th' news fr'm th' Ph'lippeens?

MR. DOOLEY, *with a wave of his hand*
Aw, that's all over.

MR. HENNESSEY, *surprised*
All over?

MR. DOOLEY, *nodding, with a sweeping gesture*
All over.

34
Manila

A CORRESPONDENT *stands alone.*

CORRESPONDENT
The New York *Evening Post*, January, 1901. I have recently
talked with a highly placed army officer, whose name I with-
hold to avoid censorship of this report. This is what he told
me.

It is openly and repeatedly asserted by army officers in Manila
that the American army is on the defensive, and that it has
been on the defensive for months.

It was on the defensive when General Otis retired and went
home to tell the people that "the situation is well in hand."
Perhaps the official code of ethics forbade his successor, General MacArthur, from discrediting that statement until after
the election. Now General MacArthur flatly states that the

127

reelection of the President will not, after all, as we were told, end the war.

The country is "pacified," the officer states sardonically, but in every town occupied by our troops and governed by "loyal" native officials it is presently discovered that a separate, secret government is being operated in behalf of the guerrillas in the field. Two thirds of our garrisons are in a state of actual siege. There are towns within a few miles of Manila where authorities will not permit an American to go, for fear he will be massacred.

The time has come when something radical must be done. At least a hundred thousand soldiers are required. General MacArthur is a good executive, but the conditions need a determined leader who will make the Filipinos lay down their arms and accept the only government that can rule them — power.

That is what army officers are saying in Manila today.

ACT THREE

1

The Pacification of the Philippines

Stygian darkness. Silence. In a pool of light stand three American GENERALS *flanked by* AIDES. *A title appears.*

THE ORDERS OF THE GENERALS

FIRST AIDE

Brigadier General James Franklin Bell, District of Southern Luzon, Commanding.

GENERAL BELL

To combat a hostile population, it is necessary to make the state of war as insupportable as possible by keeping the minds of the people in such a state of anxiety and apprehension that living under such conditions will soon become unbearable. The policy to be enforced shall be rigid and relentless.

SECOND AIDE

Order of Reconcentration.

FIRST AIDE, *reading*

"To put an end to enforced contributions now levied by insurgents upon the population, there shall be plainly marked limits surrounding each town . . ."

SECOND AIDE, *reading*
"All able-bodied males found outside the protected zones will be killed or captured."

FIRST AIDE
Order of Confiscation of Food.

SECOND AIDE, *reading*
"All rice and food supplies will be transported within the zone of protection, or burned or otherwise destroyed."

FIRST AIDE
Order of Destruction of Property.

SECOND AIDE, *reading*
"All property or merchandise found outside the zone of protection is liable to confiscation or destruction."

GENERAL BELL
Commanding officers are warned against beginning to issue food gratuitously to the civilian population until want and privation absolutely necessitate it.

FIRST AIDE
Brigadier General Jacob H. Smith, Island of Samar, Department of the Visayas, Commanding.

GENERAL SMITH, *pacing up and down*
I want no prisoners! I want you to kill and burn! The more you kill and burn the better you will please me! I want the interior of Samar made a howling wilderness. I want all persons killed who are capable of bearing arms against the United

States. Burn anything that stands, shoot anything that moves . . .

FIRST AIDE
At what age would you judge a native capable of bearing arms against the United States?

GENERAL SMITH
Anyone over ten!

SECOND AIDE
Order of Retaliation.

FIRST AIDE, *reading*
"Henceforth whenever unarmed or defenseless Americans are murdered or assassinated for political reasons, it is the policy of the brigadier general to execute a prisoner of war."

SECOND AIDE
Method of Selecting Prisoner of War.

FIRST AIDE, *reading*
"The prisoner of war to be executed will be selected by lot from among the prominent citizens held as prisoners of war, and will be chosen, when practicable, from those who belong to the town where the murder or assassination occurred."

GENERAL SMITH
No person should be given credit for loyalty solely on account of his having done nothing for or against us. The inhabitant who is not an active friend is an enemy. Neutrality will not be tolerated.

Spotlights rake the darkness. The faces of many SOLDIERS *and* OFFICERS *are seen. Two* CORRESPONDENTS *stand at the periphery. A title appears.*

131

A pale-faced CORPORAL *steps forward.*

FIRST CORRESPONDENT
Corporal Richard T. O'Brien, Twenty-sixth Infantry Volunteers.

O'BRIEN
I want to say what happened at the village of La Nog.

We entered the town just at daybreak. Word passed along the line that there would be no prisoners taken. It was sort of an unwritten law there. We were to shoot everything we saw.

The first thing we saw was a boy coming down the mountain on a water buffalo. The first sergeant shot at the boy, then we all did. That brought the people in the houses out, brought them to the door and out into the street.

The villagers offered no offense, didn't display a weapon. Two old men, carrying a white flag, and clasping hands like two brothers, approached the lines. Their hair was white. They fairly tottered, they were so old and feeble. They were shot down in their tracks. One of them was shot behind the ear, and it just lifted the roof of his head off.

A sick man appeared at the doorway of his house. He got a bullet in the abdomen and fell down in the doorway.

SERGEANT
They have various ways of getting information. Once I saw a native stripped to the waist and tied up so that only the tips of his toes touched the ground. A detachment of soldiers gathered around him and burnt his body with cigars to make

him tell where the bodies of five ambushed Americans were hid.

PRIVATE
In some cases, natives are suspended by their fingers or hung from trees and fires kindled under them.

SERGEANT
When officers really want to impress the natives, they use a form of torture known as progressive wounding. The prisoners are bound and shot in the legs. If they do not confess or die, they are shot again the following day. This is kept up from day to day until they die, but three days is usually the limit.

SECOND CORRESPONDENT, *interviewing a* CAPTAIN
An investigation is being made in the town of Laoag, as to the death beatings of natives by orders of Lieutenant Colonel Howze of the Thirty-fourth Infantry. Thirty sworn affidavits have been gathered. Your affidavit relates facts in one of these cases, Captain?

CAPTAIN
Yes. A year ago Laoag was attacked, and Lieutenant Colonel Howze arrested two prominent Filipinos, mayors of neighboring towns, for questioning. These prisoners replied that they knew nothing about the attack. They then were beaten in a manner inaugurated by the colonel.

They were laid face down on a bench in the municipal building. Whippers stood on both sides of the bench — three on a side — using rattan rods about three quarters of an inch thick, and five feet long, with which they flailed the prisoners, using all their force at every blow, so that the buttocks were gashed and the trousers shredded.

On another occasion I saw twenty natives thus stretched out, bleeding and unable to rise.

SECOND CORRESPONDENT

What happened to the two mayors?

CAPTAIN

They were beaten so hard that bits of flesh were scattered about the floor. When they were led back to jail, they could only take steps of three inches at a time, and left bloody tracks when they walked.

The following day they were questioned and beaten again. On the third day, they both died.

FIRST CORRESPONDENT

I have been reliably told that on one occasion, our soldiers took as prisoners people who held up their hands and peacefully surrendered, and an hour later, without an atom of evidence to show that they were even insurrectos, stood them on a bridge and shot them down one by one, to float downstream as examples to those who found their corpses.

SECOND CORRESPONDENT, *to the* **SERGEANT**

When a town was burned, how much notice was given to the inhabitants?

SERGEANT

We burned the town of Igbaras. It had a population of ten thousand. We burned Tigbauan. It had a population of twelve thousand. We just cried out in the streets that we would burn the town, and then we did it.

SECOND CORRESPONDENT

Were the people given time to remove their furniture?

SERGEANT
They don't have much furniture.

SECOND CORRESPONDENT
To save their personal possessions then?

SERGEANT
They only had time to save the clothes they had on.

PRIVATE, *stepping forward*
The ordinary form of torture is known as the water cure. The native is thrown on his back, his mouth pried open with a bayonet, and water is poured into his throat, filling the stomach, lungs, and intestines until he swells up like a toad.

Then he is trampled on, and the water forced from the mouth, nose, and eyes, and even the ears. Sometimes kerosene or coconut oil are used instead of water, or salt or sand are added to the solution, but the effect is the same.

FIRST CORRESPONDENT
Private A. F. Miller, Thirty-second Infantry Volunteers.

MILLER, *stolidly*
A sergeant told me he had seen the water cure taken by at least two or three hundred natives, as many as twenty sometimes in a day.

FIRST CORRESPONDENT
How are the victims selected?

MILLER
We would go out on a hike, catch a nigger, and ask him if he had a gun. He would make us a polite bow and say, "no sabby." Then we would take hold of him and give him the water cure, after which we would get two or three guns.

FIRST CORRESPONDENT, *stepping forward*

On the tenth of April, Private Andrew K. Weir of the Fourth Cavalry wrote a letter to his uncle which subsequently came to light. In it, he charged officers of his regiment with outrageous cruelty to Filipino soldiers.

For example, according to Weir one officer cut a strip of flesh from the ankle of a prisoner, attached it to a piece of wood, and coiled the flesh about the wood.

Weir says he complained to his lieutenant about the cruelty he had witnessed, and the officer replied, "These niggers have no feelings other than physical, and should not be treated as human beings."

A *handsome young* MAN *in well-tailored civilian clothing steps forward.*

SECOND CORRESPONDENT

First Lieutenant Grover Flint, formerly, Thirty-fifth Infantry.

FLINT

I returned from the Philippines some months ago. I am presently engaged in writing a biography of my late father-in-law, the historian John Fiske.

I witnessed quite a number of cases of the water cure in 1900. I regarded my duty as being to prevent anything that was excessive. For instance, in the case of very old men being given the water cure, I have seen their teeth fall out. Or sometimes a bayonet used to hold the mouth open would cut the mouth if the cure was given roughly. A man suffers tremendously, there is no doubt of it. It is like drowning. But it seemed to cause no permanent harm.

SECOND CORRESPONDENT

You did not attempt to stop our troops from administering the torture?

FLINT

No, I did not. At the time I think I did not disapprove of the procedure. To suggest that there was any impropriety would have been a suggestion against our very presence in that country.

Corporal O'BRIEN, the veteran of La Nog, is suddenly agitated.

O'BRIEN

I suppose you might call me an emotional kind of man. In civilian life, I am an actor, on the stage. And it wasn't as if I wasn't shooting at these people, too. I was, but I was horrified. They were just pursuing people and killing them on the spot!

At the other end of the town we heard screams. They had started to burn the town. There was a woman there. Her home had just been set on fire. This woman was burning up, and in her arms was a baby, and on the floor was another child, clinging to her skirts. The baby was at her breast — he was just a few months old — and this child on the floor was maybe three years of age.

FIRST CORRESPONDENT

Did anyone move to rescue her?

O'BRIEN

The house was a common bamboo shack. It was in a mass of flames.

defending himself
We were following the captain's orders. He was generally known as a nigger hater. That is the expression used.

SECOND CORRESPONDENT *is standing with a tall and impressive* OFFICER.

SECOND CORRESPONDENT

Major Cornelius Gardener, Governor, Tayabas Province. Major, you are in command of the civil government of Tayabas?

GARDENER

I am. I regret that my duty impels me, as an officer of the army, to state that the military course now being pursued in this and neighboring provinces is sowing the seeds for a perpetual revolution.

Outrages against natives are often not punished.

Almost without exception, soldiers, and also many officers, refer to the natives in their presence as "niggers," and the natives are beginning to understand what "nigger" means . . .

A BLACK SOLDIER *comes forward.*

BLACK SOLDIER

I have recently returned home from the Philippines. I was in the Ninth Cavalry. I was struck by a question a little native boy asked me, which ran about this way. "Why does the American Negro come from America to fight us when we are much friend to him and have not done anything to him? He is all the same as me, and me all the same as you. Why don't you fight those people in America that burn the Negroes, that made a beast of you, that took the child from its mother's side and sold it?"

I was staggered, and could make no reply. But some men from my company, they deserted and joined the Filipinos . . .

138

The stage lapses into darkness. In a solitary light, the third GEN-
ERAL *stands, relaxed, pleasant, reasonable.*

AIDE

Commanding General Adna R. Chaffee, successor in these islands to General MacArthur.

CHAFFEE

The United States government, disregarding many provoca-
tions to do otherwise, has for three years exercised an extraordinary forbearance and patiently adhered to a magnanimous
policy toward the inhabitants of these islands.

This government's kindliest efforts at pacification have been
arrogantly interpreted as an evidence of weakness and fear.
What is needed now is the wholesome fear by these people of
the American army.

We are dealing with a people who are absolutely hostile to
the white race, who regard life as of little value, and who will
not submit to our control until absolutely whipped into such
a condition. Any means to that end is advisable.

While I do not urge inhuman treatment of any person, a short
and severe war creates in the aggregate less loss and suffering
than benevolent war, indefinitely prolonged.

2

A Garden in Manila

JULIANA LOPEZ, *a refined and spirited Philippine woman of
twenty-three, is writing a letter to her sister.*

JULIANA
Dearest Sister Clemencia,

In your letter you advise me to practice on the piano. I am
sorry I cannot please you, but our piano was a rented one, and
as soon as the Americans arrested our brothers, I sent it back.
I am hardly in a mood for playing, and it was costing us twelve
dollars a month, which is too much luxury for us these days.

I pray that your visit to America to see the President and arrange the release of our brothers has been successful. They
keep demanding fifty guns from Cipriano, but when he surrendered with his men he turned in every gun they had. I
told the American authorities that if they keep Cipriano in
prison until they get the fifty guns, they ought to authorize the
family to buy the guns abroad, as it will not be possible to
obtain them here!

pulling a long face
They looked serious when I told them that, but I don't care
what the Americans think — it is the truth!

So many incredible and horrible things have happened. The
foremen of our farms have been arrested and beaten. In
Batangas this General Bell says he will devastate the province
if it is not pacified at once. In some outlying places, the
Americans obliged the householders to walk on foot from the
town, each one carrying a tin can of petroleum, and when they
arrived, each was required to burn his own house! Luna's
father, after incredible torture, was thrown still alive on the
fire because his son is an insurgent and he had not been able
to bring about his surrender.

If you could hear us talk at home now about these invaders
it would astonish you, for before all this happened, who would
have believed that the Americans could take such measures,

considering that they boast all over the world wherever they go of their humane and civilized acts! They will go to any length to bring about peace. But they will never have moral peace, only physical. I, for my part, will never forget these offenses!

Take care in writing to us. Write nothing of politics, if you do not wish to make our situation worse. Even in Manila, no one lives safely.

Your devoted sister, Juliana Lopez.

3
Faneuil Hall, Boston

Voices are heard, "We demand the truth! We demand the truth!" Headlines.

PROTESTS MOUNT AGAINST WAR CONDUCT

MASS MEETINGS HELD IN BOSTON
Moorfield Storey Addresses Citizens
Demanding Public Inquiry

Storey, an anti-imperialist, is a prominent Boston attorney. His voice shakes with intensity. Above him hangs a banner carrying a defiant inscription.

FIAT LUX

MASS MEETING AGAINST THE
SUPPRESSION OF THE TRUTH
ABOUT THE PHILIPPINES

We know now we have been deceived! That statements made to us for years as to the beginnings of the war — the feelings of the Philippine people, the extent and nature of the struggle, the manner in which it was conducted — were not true!

The truth is buried in the archives of the War Department!

Applause

We demand the truth about reconcentration of citizens, killing of prisoners, shooting of suspected persons, the use of torture —

The chant resumes, "We demand the truth."

The exact truth must now be laid before the people of the United States!

Tumultuous applause. Headlines.

HUNDREDS PETITION SENATE URGING INVESTIGATION OF ATROCITY CHARGES

PROMINENT CLERGY ASK ADMINISTRATION TO ACT

4
The United States Senate

Among those present are HOAR *and* TILLMAN, LODGE *and* SPOONER. *Each side of the Philippine question has gained new strength. Freshman Senator* EDWARD CARMACK, *Tennessee Democrat, is outspoken against the war.* ALBERT

Beveridge, *Republican of Indiana, a senator since 1899, has become a major voice for the imperialist policy.*

Hoar, *holding a petition in his hands*
This concern has reached the American people. This petition for an investigation is signed by citizens of unquestioned patriotism — Mr. Mark Twain, William Dean Howells, Professor William James, Professor John Dewey. Thirty-six professors from the University of Chicago alone.

Beveridge
The appropriate committee to hold such an investigation would be the Committee on the Philippines under Chairman Lodge.

Tillman *hoots derisively.*

Lodge
The petition should be directed by the Senate to the Committee on the Philippines.

Carmack *stands. He is brilliant, impatient, and precise. He speaks with a Tennessee drawl.*

Carmack
I suppose that the Senate, following the suggestion of the Senator from Indiana, will send the petition to the Committee on the Philippines. I suppose also that every senator thoroughly understands that you might as well write a letter to a dead man as to send a petition of this nature to that committee — I am on it. I should know!

Beveridge
So am I, sir!

CARMACK

However, before the document goes to its grave, I wish to make a few remarks concerning the remains.

BEVERIDGE

Mr. President, who has the floor?

PRESIDING OFFICER

Mr. Hoar has the floor.

HOAR

Mr. President, I yield to my new colleague from Tennessee. I am in an uncomfortable position as to health today. The able gentleman will carry on where I may falter.

PRESIDING OFFICER

Mr. Carmack has the floor.

CARMACK

I thank the Senator. The point to which I wish to direct the attention of the Senate is that while all these horrors have been steadily going on for months and years, while the story of them has been pouring in upon this country all the time, there has been absolutely no effort on the part of the Administration or of the War Department to put an end to them, but every effort to conceal or deny them.

There has been a conspiracy for the suppression of truth and for the dissemination of falsehood in regard to the affairs of the Philippine Islands.

BEVERIDGE, *jumping up*

That is an outrageous falsehood!

TILLMAN

Is it denied that these things, or some of them, have been proved, and that no man has yet been punished?

HOAR, *half rising from his seat*

I cannot help believe that not a twentieth part of the story has yet been told. I get letters in large numbers from officers testifying to these cruelties.

SPOONER, *addressing* CARMACK

On the contrary, Senator, I think you will find that the War Department and Secretary of War Root have been exceedingly diligent in hunting down all unfortunate instances of this kind in the Philippines.

CARMACK

Oh yes, the department has been diligent. But not to avoid guilt, sir, only to avoid shame. They are not trying to suppress crime, but to suppress the knowledge of it from the American people!

LODGE, *wearily*

I confess I am growing tired of these ceaseless attacks by our southern colleagues on the other side of the chamber.

gazing directly at TILLMAN *and* CARMACK

They have developed a highly commendable if somewhat hysterical tenderness for the rights of men with dark skins dwelling in the islands of the Pacific, in pleasing contrast to the harsh indifference which they manifest toward black American citizens.

This triggers TILLMAN *like an alarm.*

TILLMAN, *wagging a finger at* LODGE

Oh no, we are not going to run off after the foxes just now!

Do not charge us with hypocrisy when I can see the hypocrite oozing out of you all over! We have in the United States a race problem which will give you scope for all the elevating and christianizing of which you are capable, yet you turn your backs on that and march to the East (*stabbing at* LODGE *and* BEVERIDGE *with his finger*) and you murder, you butcher, you shoot them in blood, you torture them, you do everything! You have eclipsed the South, and you have done it all in three years.

So we are not going to run after the foxes. We are after this Filipino coon and we want his hide! We want you to vindicate your policy. We want you to exonerate the American army!

BEVERIDGE, *rising to the challenge*
The opposition denounces the whole American army because out of one hundred thirty thousand soldiers a dozen have proved derelict!

CARMACK, *howling*
A dozen, sir!

BEVERIDGE
We do not scuttle a ship because it has barnacles!

In the long sweep and historical survey of this large business, we must dominate in the Pacific. These gentlemen who cry for freedom in the Philippines might reflect that Cuban independence was an error, and one we have begun to rectify.

A *commotion in the chamber.* CARMACK *regards* BEVERIDGE *with silent contempt.*

CARMACK
The plain truth of the matter is that senators upon the other side of the chamber know of the awful horrors that are being

enacted in our Philippine War, but they do not care. It is not even a topic of conversation!

Of course the Senator from Indiana and others (*looking at* BEVERIDGE) are eloquent in their appeals for the friendly natives. They say we on this side of the chamber are thinking all the time of the welfare of the hostile Filipino —

LODGE
If I may correct the Senator, I believe I said that to leave the islands now would be a grave dereliction of duty, a base betrayal of the Filipinos who have supported us, led by the best men of Luzon —

CARMACK
Chaffee and Bell and Smith out there declare that there are no friendly Filipinos! The plain truth is that you have been waging a war of indiscriminate ferocity against a whole people, without seeking to make any distinction whatever between combatants and noncombatants, between friends and foes.

Make the land a howling wilderness! Put everybody above ten years of age to the sword!

bearing down upon the opposition
And these barbarities, sir, have not been perpetrated, as has been weakly suggested, by way of retaliation. They have not been perpetrated for punishment or even for revenge. It is a cold-blooded, calculated cruelty. It is simply part of a war waged upon the principle of making its horrors so vast and so universal that the whole people will cry for peace, or else there will be no man left to prosecute the war!

CARMACK *sits abruptly, and turns away. There is a moment of fraught silence. Then* HOAR, *rising with difficulty, begins to speak very quietly.*

147

The Secretary of the Province of Batangas in the Philippine Islands has reported that one third of the three hundred thousand population of that province have died within two years.

fumbling for a clipping
The *New York Times* quotes an interview with General Bell in which he said that one sixth of the natives of Luzon alone have been killed or died of dengue fever — which I suppose is the direct result of war, and comes from the condition of starvation brought on by war — and that this has happened in the last two years.

One sixth of the population of Luzon is upward of half a million people. If this be true, we have caused the death of more human beings in the Philippines than we have caused to our enemies in all our other wars put together, including the terrible Civil War. These figures have been nowhere denied.

The general in the interview approves the policy. "The loss of life by killing alone has been very great," he concedes. "But I think not one man has been slain except where his death served the legitimate purposes of war."

shaking his head
What can we say?

He contemplates the degradation of the country. He has no answer.
What have we to say?

We are not talking of the ordinary brutalities of war. We are talking about concentration camps, we are talking about killing the wounded, we are talking about torture, we are talking about orders from high authority to depopulate whole districts and to slay all inhabitants, including all boys over ten years old.

What have we to say?

I do not deny that you will get peace pretty soon. You will get pretended submission. But the volcano will be there. The lava will break out again. You will never settle this thing until you settle it aright!

It may be that the battle for this day is lost. But I have an assured faith in the justice and the love of liberty of the American people. If the battle today go against it, I appeal to another day, not distant, and sure to come.

I appeal from the clapping of hands and the stamping of feet and the brawling and the shouting to the quiet chamber of the fathers in Philadelphia. I appeal from the spirit of trade to the spirit of liberty. I appeal from the empire to the republic.

I appeal from the millionaire and the boss and the wire-puller and the manager, to the statesman of the elder time, who lived and died poor, and who left to his children and to his countrymen a good name, better than riches.

I appeal from the present, bloated with material prosperity, drunk with the lust of empire, to another and a better age. I appeal from the Present to the Future, and to the Past.

Darkness. We hear the chanting of the Catholic solemn Mass of the Dead.

> *Dies irae, dies illa,*
> *Solvet saeclum in favilla . . .*

5

Church of the Immaculate Conception, Montclair, New Jersey

REPORTER

A solemn High Mass of Requiem for the repose of the souls of the Filipinos who have died fighting for their country was sung in the Church of the Immaculate Conception this morning, in Montclair, New Jersey.

The Mass was in the nature of a protest against the acts of the American government in the Philippine Islands.

He turns to Reverend JOSEPH MENDL, *a Catholic priest.*

Reverend Mendl, do all your parishioners agree with your position on the war in the Philippines?

MENDL

My people are behind me. And the few who aren't are political jackasses!

The singing of the Mass continues.

6

The White House

President MCKINLEY *confides in the audience.*

MCKINLEY

The truth is, I didn't want the Philippines. And when we received the cable from Admiral Dewey saying he took the islands, I couldn't have told you where that darned place was within two thousand miles.

I didn't know what to do with them. I sought counsel from all sides — Democrats as well as Republicans — but got little help.

I thought first we would only take Manila. Then Luzon. Then other islands perhaps, also. I walked the floor of the White House night after night until midnight. And I am not ashamed to tell you, my friends, that I went down on my knees and prayed to Almighty God for light and guidance more than one night.

And then one night, it came to me this way — I don't know how it was, but it came — that we could not give them back to Spain: that would be cowardly and dishonorable. That we could not turn them over to France or Germany, our commercial rivals in the Orient: that would be bad business. That we could not leave them to themselves: they would soon have anarchy and misrule over there worse than Spain's was.

And that there was nothing left for us to do but to take them all, and to educate the Filipinos, and uplift and civilize and christianize them, and by God's grace, to do the best we could by them.

And then I went to bed and went to sleep and slept soundly. And the next morning I sent for the chief engineer of the War Department — the official map maker — and I told him to put the Philippines on the map of the United States.

And there they are. And there they will stay, while I am President!

Two shots ring out. McKINLEY *looks stricken and falls.* PEOPLE *run to his assistance. The stage is plunged in darkness.* VOICES *cry out —* "The President! The President is shot!"

A police bell sounds, and then clangs steadily. Lights flash on and off. We see, in brief flashes of illumination, HANNA *on his knees at the President's side,* LODGE *covering his eyes in grief,* HAY *groping blindly for his handkerchief. There is the sound of grown men weeping. Headlines.*

SEPTEMBER 7, 1901

P R E S I D E N T M c K I N L E Y S H O T
A T B U F F A L O E X P O S I T I O N

WOUNDED TWICE BY POLISH ANARCHIST

NATION PRAYS FOR HIS RECOVERY

WEEK-LONG FIGHT FOR LIFE IS ENDED

T H E P R E S I D E N T I S D E A D

The mourners lower their heads and stand in silence. HANNA, *pained and angry, his face stained with tears, walks aside.*

HANNA
  I told them not to nominate Roosevelt. And now that god-damned cowboy is President of the United States!

7
"The White House Blues"

A song, sung by a GROUP *of four.*

GROUP

 Roosevelt's in the White House, doing his best,
 McKinley's in the graveyard, taking his rest,
 Gonna be gone long time, long time.

 Roosevelt's in the White House, eating with a silver spoon,
 McKinley's in the graveyard, meeting his doom,
 Gonna be gone long time, long time.

 Roosevelt's in the White House, drinking from a silver cup,
 McKinley's in the graveyard, he'll never wake up,
 Gonna be gone long time, long time.

8
The Hearings

In a Senate committee room, two WITNESSES *in witness chairs, each before a microphone. Bright lights are on the affable and corpulent* WILLIAM HOWARD TAFT.

TAFT

It is my deliberate judgment that there never was a war conducted, whether against inferior races or not, in which there were more compassion and more restraint and more generosity — assuming there was a war at all — than there have been in the Philippine Islands.

FEBRUARY 1, 1902

SENATE COMMITTEE ON THE PHILIPPINES STARTS INQUIRY

CHAIRMAN LODGE PROMISES THOROUGH INVESTIGATION

FIRST WITNESS IS WILLIAM HOWARD TAFT, PHILIPPINE CIVIL GOVERNOR

TAFT, *continuing*

Now I say that having been only in Manila, of course, but I talked with officers of the army there, and knew what the general policy was.

It is true of course in individual instances that cruelties have been inflicted.

laughing genially

There are some rather amusing instances of Filipinos who came in and said they would not say anything until they were tortured — that they must have an excuse for what they proposed to say!

sternly

It seems clear that a great majority of the people are restrained by fear from assisting in the suppression of the insurrection. Anyone suspected of aiding the Americans is marked for assassination. They burn them alive and throw them into wells. It is a terrorism of an entire people. It is a Mafia on a very large scale.

In the other witness chair, General HUGHES *begins to testify. His name card is posted on the roster.*

BRIGADIER GENERAL ROBERT P. HUGHES
COMMANDER, DEPARTMENT OF THE VISAYAS,
DIVISION OF THE PHILIPPINES

HUGHES

As for the so-called water cure, I never heard of it. I did not know what it was.

I have read a paper since I came home, emanating from Boston, describing it, and I can assure you the thing was not practiced under my command.

As for shooting down natives after they had ceased to fight, I never knew of any case of that kind in all my two years and a half in the islands.

Of course the policy became stiffer as we went along, and it is no doubt true that the punishment would fall partly on the women and children. But women and children are part of the family, and where you wish to inflict a punishment, you can punish the man probably worse in that way than in any other.

regretfully
It is not civilized warfare, but these people are not civilized.

FREDERICK FUNSTON *rises from the other witness chair and heatedly defends the army. His name appears on the roster.*

BRIGADIER GENERAL FREDERICK FUNSTON

FUNSTON

A soldier who claims to have been with me in the Philippines told this committee that he helped to administer the "water cure" to 160 natives, of whom only 26 lived.

155

That statement I wish to brand as an atrocious lie, without the slightest foundation in fact!

During my service of three years in the Philippines I never had personal knowledge of the so-called water cure being administered to a native, or any other form of torture to extract information from them. Statements of this kind made by returned soldiers are simply braggadocio, and a desire to attract attention to themselves.

Colonel WAGNER *stands before a map display, showing secure and enemy territory in recalcitrant provinces. His name appears on the roster.*

COLONEL ARTHUR L. WAGNER
ASSISTANT ADJUTANT GENERAL

WAGNER

In regard to these camps of reconcentration . . . The condition of our military forces before we had these camps might be compared to a blind giant — strong, but unable to see.

The troops were more than able to annihilate, to completely smash, the insurgents — if we could find them — but it was impossible to get any information.

By bringing all these people within the reconcentration camps, we were able to separate our friends from our enemies. Everything beyond the limits was an enemy.

At the same time, these people had (*generously*) complete personal liberty in the camps — as long as they stayed within the limits, within what we call the dead line. They could go up to 300 yards from the camp.

In the other chair appears the final witness, General MacArthur. *His name card is posted on the roster.*

Major General Arthur MacArthur
FORMER MILITARY GOVERNOR OF
THE PHILIPPINE ISLANDS

MacArthur

In my opinion, American possession of the Philippine Islands is likely to transcend in importance anything that has happened since Columbus discovered America.

You see, all other governments have gone to the East simply to plant trading establishments. There is not a single such establishment in my judgment in Asia today that would survive five years if the original power which planted it was withdrawn.

But we are planting something that cannot be destroyed. We are implanting the imperishable ideas of Americanism. We are implanting a thing that can never be removed from that soil. That seems to me a most inspiring thought.

Certainly some of our soldiers have committed excesses under provocation of hardship. But I doubt if any war on earth has been conducted with as much humanity, as much self-restraint — in view of the character of the adversary — as have been our operations in the Philippine Islands. It has been the most legitimate and humane war ever conducted on the face of this earth.

9
The Court-Martials

Three high-ranking Officers *sit on a bench. Below, and at either side, a* Clerk, *and a* Prosecutor.

Reporter
Washington. Though one could wish that President Roosevelt had acted before the aroused conscience of the people practically forced action, it is a welcome sign that the horror and indignation of the country have stirred up his tardy Administration at last.

It is now said that the President is determined to sift to the bottom charges of cruelty in the Philippines, nothing being concealed, no man being for any reason favored or shielded.

The Clerk *reads the names of the accused, the* Prosecutor *reads the charges. The cases follow one another without a break.*

Clerk
Major Edwin F. Glenn, Fifth U.S. Infantry.

First Officer
Charge.

Prosecutor
Conduct to the prejudice of good order and military discipline.

Second Officer
Specification.

Prosecutor
Accused did execute a method of punishment commonly known as the "water cure" . . .

158

SECOND OFFICER
   Of the Specification.

THIRD OFFICER
   Guilty.

FIRST OFFICER
   Of the Charge.

THIRD OFFICER
   Guilty.

FIRST OFFICER
   Suspended from command for the period of one month.

SECOND OFFICER
   And in addition a fine of fifty dollars.

CLERK
   First Lieutenant Julien E. Gaugot, Tenth U.S. Cavalry.

FIRST OFFICER
   Charge.

PROSECUTOR
   Conduct to the prejudice of good order and military discipline.

SECOND OFFICER
   Specification.

PROSECUTOR
   Accused caused soldiers in his command to execute method of
   punishment known as the "water cure" . . .

SECOND OFFICER
   Of the Specification.

THIRD OFFICER
Guilty.

FIRST OFFICER
Of the Charge.

THIRD OFFICER
Guilty.

SECOND OFFICER
Suspended from command for a period of three months.

FIRST OFFICER
And in addition a fine of fifty dollars per month for the same period.

CLERK
First Lieutenant Edwin A. Hickman, First U.S. Cavalry.

FIRST OFFICER
Charge.

PROSECUTOR
Conduct to the prejudice of good order and military discipline.

SECOND OFFICER
Specification.

PROSECUTOR
Accused did unlawfully order and direct soldiers in his command to seize and immerse natives in water for the purpose of extorting information.

SECOND OFFICER
Of the Specification.

Third Officer
Guilty.

Second Officer
Except the word "unlawfully."

First Officer
Of the Charge.

Third Officer
Not guilty.

Second Officer
Acquitted.

Clerk
First Lieutenant Preston Brown, Second U.S. Infantry.

First Officer
Charge.

Prosecutor
Murder.

Second Officer
Specification.

Prosecutor
Accused did willfully and feloniously shoot and murder unresisting native.

Second Officer
Of the Specification.

Third Officer
Guilty.

First Officer
Except the word "feloniously."

Second Officer
Of the Charge.

Third Officer
Guilty.

First Officer
Except the word "murder," substituting "manslaughter."

Second Officer
Loss of thirty files in lineal rank on the list of first lieutenants.

Third Officer
Fine of one-half monthly pay for a period of nine months.

Clerk
First Lieutenant John Horace Arthur Day, U.S. Marine Corps.

First Officer
Charge.

Prosecutor
Murder.

Second Officer
Specification.

Prosecutor
Accused did willfully and feloniously with malice aforethought murder and kill eleven natives of the Philippine Islands, names unknown, by ordering and causing enlisted men to shoot said natives to death with rifles.

SECOND OFFICER
  Of the Specification.

THIRD OFFICER
  Not guilty.

FIRST OFFICER
  Of the Charge.

THIRD OFFICER
  Not guilty.

Accused showed that he executed said natives in obedience to the orders of his immediate commanding officer, Major Littleton W. T. Waller.

CLERK
  Major Littleton W. T. Waller, U.S. Marine Corps.

FIRST OFFICER
  Charge.

PROSECUTOR
  Murder.

SECOND OFFICER
  Specification.

PROSECUTOR
  Accused did willfully and feloniously and with malice aforethought murder and kill eleven natives of the Philippine Islands, names unknown, by ordering and causing subordinate officers subject to his command to shoot said natives to death with rifles.

Second Officer
Of the Specification.

Third Officer
Guilty.

First Officer
Except the words "willfully and feloniously and with malice aforethought."

Second Officer
Of the Charge.

Third Officer
Not guilty.

Accused testified that he was governed entirely by instructions of his immediate commanding officer to "take no prisoners" and to "kill and burn" and to leave the interior of Samar a "howling wilderness."

Clerk
Brigadier General Jacob H. Smith, United States Army.

First Officer
Charge.

Prosecutor
Conduct to the prejudice of good order and military discipline.

Second Officer
Specification.

Prosecutor
Accused did give instructions to his subordinate officer, Major L. W. T. Waller, "I want no prisoners" (meaning thereby that

giving of quarter was not desired or required), and did further give instructions that he wanted all persons killed who were capable of bearing arms and did designate the age limit as ten years of age.

SECOND OFFICER
Of the Specification.

THIRD OFFICER
Guilty.

FIRST OFFICER
Except the words "meaning thereby that giving of quarter was not desired or required."

SECOND OFFICER
Of the Charge.

THIRD OFFICER
Guilty.

FIRST OFFICER
The court does therefore sentence Brigadier General Jacob H. Smith to be admonished by the reviewing authority.

THIRD OFFICER
The court is lenient in that the accused did not mean everything that his language implied, and that the orders were never executed in such sense, and that a desperate struggle was being conducted with a cruel and savage foe.

10

The War Department

Secretary of War ELIHU ROOT *with a* REPORTER. *Army Of-*
FICERS stand behind.

REPORTER
Special to the *New York Times.* A sensation was created in
army circles today when the Secretary of War, Elihu Root,
announced the decision of the President in the court-martial
case of Brigadier General Jacob H. Smith.

General Smith is the highest-ranking American army officer
ever to be found guilty by a military tribunal.

ROOT
General Smith has behind him a long career distinguished for
gallantry and good conduct. He was wounded in the Civil
War and in the war with Spain.

He has acquired the sobriquet of "Hell-Roaring Jake" because
of the extravagance of his language, which is habitual with him,
and partly explains the charges against him.

However, the President directs that it is no longer for the
interest of the service that General Smith should continue to
exercise the command of his rank. At sixty-two, he is nearing
the age of retirement. The President directs that he be retired
from the active list to take effect this date.

The OFFICERS *gasp. One of them buttonholes the* REPORTER.

OFFICER
The President is making a political example of Smith! If the

court had had any idea that the President would exceed the sentence it would not have convicted Smith at all!

11

Sagamore Hill, the Roosevelt Estate

It is July Fourth afternoon. LODGE *and* ROOT, *guests of the President at his Long Island retreat, are in a happy mood.*

LODGE, *to* ROOT, *laughing*
Do you know what Henry Adams said about Theodore?

ROOT, *laughing*
No, what?

LODGE
"Roosevelt," he said, "more than any other man living within the range of notoriety, shows the singular, primitive quality that belongs to ultimate matter — "

ROOT, *laughing*
I like "singular," but not "primitive" —

LODGE
Wait! "He has," says Adams, "the quality that medieval theology assigned to God. He is pure Act."

They both laugh. The PRESIDENT *enters. They jump to their feet.*

TR, *genially*
What's that, Cabot? Who's attacking me now?

LODGE
Henry Adams. But I believe Henry considered it praise.

TR, *laughing*
Like Dooley. I don't know what I would do if a month went by and I wasn't attacked in Mr. Dooley's column.

ROOT, *laughing*
Oh yes, then look out!

TR
I should have to give up plans to run for a second term.

They laugh again.

LODGE
We can always arrange an attack on you by Carl Schurz and Andrew Carnegie.

ROOT
This last thing was scandalous. Now the court-martials are a farce —

LODGE
And the hearings are a whitewash. (*he shakes his head*) They want *new* hearings!

The afternoon light begins to fade. The three friends settle in for a leisurely chat.

TR
I expect nothing from that crowd. Schurz is a dog, and the rest of them have no sense of historical proportion.

After the Wounded Knee campaign twelve years ago, the perpetrators were never punished in any way. And we haven't a single incident in the Philippines as bad as the massacre at Wounded Knee.

Put that in a speech, Elihu.

ROOT, *demurring*
It will only give the impression that we're defending ourselves. Besides, people don't want to hear from the War Department. They're thinking about the tariff and the coal strike —

TR
We're going to come out all right on that!

ROOT
— and the Philippines seem to be a matter of merely historical interest.

LODGE
The press is finished with the thing. The Philippines have ceased to be an issue.

TR
Except in Boston.

They all laugh.

LODGE, *thoughtfully*
The country has lost all interest in it. I doubt it will be mentioned in the next campaign.

Lights fade to total darkness. Fireworks burst silently against the sky.

TR, *contentedly*
Ah, fireworks!

12

Peace

The word "Peace" is blazoned across the sky in a firework display. A military AIDE *steps forward.*

AIDE
The proclamation of President Theodore Roosevelt, in which general peace, amnesty, and civil government are established in the Philippine Islands, on this, the fourth day of July, nineteen hundred and two.

ROOOSEVELT *appears on a balcony.*

TR
I wish to thank the officers and enlisted men of the United States Army in the Philippines, for the indomitable spirit and loyal devotion with which they have put down and ended the great insurrection which has raged throughout the archipelago against the lawful sovereignty and just authority of the United States.

The task was peculiarly difficult and trying. They were required at first to overcome organized resistance of superior numbers, well-equipped with modern arms of precision, entrenched in unknown country of mountain defiles, jungle, and swamps, apparently capable of interminable defense.

When this resistance had been overcome, they were required to crush out a general system of guerrilla warfare, from which it was almost impossible to guard against surprise or ambush.

They were obliged to deal with problems of communication and transportation in a country without roads and frequently made impassable by torrential rains.

Widely scattered over a large archipelago extending a thousand miles from north to south, the gravest responsibilities involving the life or death of their commands frequently devolved upon young or inexperienced officers beyond the reach of specific orders or advice.

I deeply deplore to say that some among them have committed acts of cruelty. The guilty have been punished. But in punishing them, let those who sit at ease at home, who walk delicately and live in the soft places of the earth, remember also to do them common justice.

Let not the effortless and the untempted rail overmuch at strong men who with blood and sweat, and days and nights of agony, and years of toil, have risked life in remote tropic jungles to bring the light of civilization into the world's dark places.

The army has added honor to the flag, which it defended, and has justified increased confidence in the future of the American people, whose soldiers do not shrink from labor or death, yet love liberty and peace.

There is a final burst of fireworks. We hear "The Star-Spangled Banner." The PRESIDENT *stands solemnly at attention, his eyes far away in thought.*

NOTES & SOURCES

SELECTED BIBLIOGRAPHY

BIOGRAPHIES

CHRONOLOGY

NOTES AND SOURCES

The historical record as we researched and used it consisted of contemporary newspaper accounts; Congressional debates and hearings; records of the U.S. War Department; pamphlets and reports of protest meetings of the anti-imperialists; proceedings of political conventions; articles from literary and political magazines; published correspondence and reminiscences; manuscript collections of the leading figures; and secondary historical material of all kinds. This documentary material we treated as our "footage." We cut, edited, and reordered it with both history and theatre in mind.

The language of the play consists of documentary fragments taken from their immediate contexts and woven together to make a dramatic narrative. Thus a Lodge remark on treaty ratification in a letter to a newspaper editor appears in a phone conversation with Roosevelt; and a passage on the Rough Riders from the Roosevelt *Autobiography* crops up as dialogue spoken by Roosevelt in the recruitment scene.

Overwhelmingly, the language is quoted, rather than adapted, from its sources. It was necessary in some places, however, to alter slightly the words of the written record in order to make them dramatically clear and alive. Hay's remark that a treaty of peace should be ratified "with unanimity" sounded better with a simple "unanimously." Juliana Lopez's "But they will never have moral peace, only physical" is a lightening of the awkward original, "But it will not be possible for them to bring about moral peace, but only physical."

In addition, we occasionally invent interstitial language for flow or humor. Some of the exclamations are ours (A soldier's "Damn!"; Hay's "It is preposterous!") and a few tag lines which round out the sense of a documentary speech, like Platt's "Let him have the job," and Carnegie's "Business and labor, hmmm?"

Occasionally we reattributed bits of language from figures whom we were unable to include in the cast. For instance, Senator Henry Teller's comment on the domestic effect of a foreign policy "blunder" is spoken by Senator Allen, who was a better character for us because of his relationship with Bryan. Such reattributions are duly noted below.

We had to create a dramatic context for our documentary text. Very often the dramatic event corresponds to the historical event: Schurz's anti-imperialist speeches, the Senate debates, the McKinley-Kohlsaat meeting, TR's encounter with Dudley Dean are given stage equivalents of their original settings. But how is one to dramatize a letter file from the Library of Congress? Hence many of the events depicted in the play, like press conferences, street rallies, and phone calls, are inventions which galvanize the written record into speech. Personal letters are the documentary basis alike for the sleepy afternoon on the Roosevelt estate, and the frantic morning in Andrew Carnegie's study.

These NOTES will clarify the organization of the play by listing and discussing the sources we used. The section is divided into topical groupings arranged to follow the order of the scenes in the play. Following each list of sources is a brief essay that is part footnotes, part historical background, and part historiographical comment. Literal footnoting, while possible, would have been unreadable: every line would have required a citation. We do not deal with every line of the play, but believe we account for most passages of historical significance.

An exception is the material drawn from newspapers. To avoid tiresome repetition, we omitted newspaper source listings for each scene and cited newspaper sources in the essays only where we thought them especially important. The headlines, unless otherwise indicated, are either quoted directly or adapted from the following newspapers, which we read selectively for the years 1896–1902.

Boston *Evening Transcript*	New York *Evening Post*
Boston *Globe*	New York *Journal*
Boston *Herald*	New York *Sun*

Chicago *Tribune*   *New York Times*
Springfield *Republican*   New York *Tribune*
New York *World*

These papers were valuable for the documentary language they gave us and provided a basis for our understanding of key events. Many works that were not used in the play in any form were essential to our research. These include published memoirs and papers of characters in the play, reminiscences of observers, biographies of the leading figures, general studies of American imperialism and anti-imperialism, and works on Philippine history. These belong in a complete bibliography of our subject, which we have not included. We list below only those sources actually drawn upon in the play.

We offer at the end of these NOTES a short list of secondary works on various aspects of our subject that may be helpful to those wishing to read further in the field.

AMERICA, BEFORE McKINLEY ACT I: 1

Adams, Henry. *The Education of Henry Adams.* Boston, 1918.

The *Education* has been called the "single document of the great transformation of American life after the Civil War." Adams' pessimistic view of fin-de-siècle America suggests the spirit of the period as seen by its ruling elite. Some of the thoughts here refer to the crash and economic depression of the early nineties, some to the mood of the Republican eastern establishment at the time of McKinley's election a few years later.

LODGE, ROOSEVELT, AND THE ACT I: 2, 3, 5 BEGINNINGS OF AN IMPERIAL POLICY

Lang, Louis, ed. *The Autobiography of Thomas Collier Platt.* New York, 1910.

Lodge, Henry Cabot, ed. *Selections from the Correspondence of Theodore Roosevelt and Henry Cabot Lodge, 1884–1918.* 2 vols. New York, 1925. Vol. 1.

——. "Our Duty to Cuba." *The Forum,* Vol. 21 (April 1896).

Morison, Elting E., and John M. Blum. *The Letters of Theodore Roosevelt.* 8 vols. Cambridge, 1951–1954. Vol. 1.

The friendship of Roosevelt and Lodge is one of the best known in the history of American politics. Their remarkable correspondence, part of the Lodge collection at the Massachusetts Historical Society, was edited by Lodge and published as *Selections* (and very selective he was, for there are several notable omissions). It records the vicissitudes of the two friends' political careers for more than thirty years and is the basic source for the Roosevelt-Lodge scenes throughout, whether used in its original form or as dialogue. The Roosevelt Papers at the Library of Congress and Morison and Blum's excellent collection of Roosevelt letters were other useful sources for these scenes.

When the play opens, Lodge was already one of the Senate's leading spokesmen on foreign affairs. His views on the need for an aggressive new foreign policy were shared, and in part shaped, by Roosevelt.

Lodge described his postelection meeting with McKinley in a letter to Roosevelt in the *Selections*. His comment on the Cleveland administration and Cuba comes from his *Forum* article.

Roosevelt's remarks in Scene 3 on the bombardment of the seacoast cities are taken from two letters to Lodge and one to his friend Cecil Spring Rice that predate McKinley's election by a few months to a year. They are used here to suggest Roosevelt's general bellicosity in foreign affairs and his long-standing views on naval preparedness. His Scene 5 material is from the *Selections* and Morison.

Platt's comment ("I don't particularly like Theodore") is taken from his authored, and not altogether reliable, "autobiography."

CONDITIONS IN CUBA   ACT I: 4, 6

Congressional Record, 55 Cong., 2 sess.

Remington, Frederic. "The Sorrows of Don Tomas Pidal, A Reconcentrado." *Harper's New Monthly Magazine,* Vol. 99 (August 1899).

Historians have called the speech of the respected Vermont Senator Proctor on his return from Cuba in early 1898 one of the most influential in the history of the Senate. The speech validated sensational newspaper accounts of Spanish atrocities against the native population to even the most reluctant and skeptical observers. It unquestionably moved Congress closer to war with Spain.

Parts of the speech, along with material from the New York World, were used for the correspondents' exposition of the Cuban situation in Scene 4.

Don Tomas Pidal told his painful story to war correspondents Sylvester Scovel and Frederic Remington in a *fonda* (restaurant) in Havana province.

WAR FEVER   ACT I: 7–13

Allen, Gardener, ed. "Papers of John Davis Long, 1897–1904." *The Massachusetts Historical Society Collections*. Vol. 78 (1939).

Bailey, Thomas A. *A Diplomatic History of the American People*. New York, 1940.

Beer, Thomas. *Hanna*. New York, 1929.

Brown, Charles H. *The Correspondents' War*. New York, 1967.

Congressional Record, 65 Cong., 3 sess.

Dewey, George. *The Autobiography of George Dewey, Admiral of the Navy*. New York, 1913.

Garraty, John A. *Henry Cabot Lodge*. New York, 1953.

Hagedorn, Hermann. *The Rough Riders: A Romance*. New York, 1923.

Kohlsaat, Herman H. *From McKinley to Harding*. New York, 1923.

Lodge. *Selections from the Roosevelt-Lodge Correspondence*. Vol. 1.

Long, Margaret, ed. *The Journal of John D. Long*. Rindge, N.H., 1956.

May, Ernest R. *Imperial Democracy*. New York, 1961.

Mayo, Lawrence Shaw, ed. *America of Yesterday as Reflected in the Journal of John Davis Long*. Boston, 1923.

Miller, Marion M., ed. *Great Debates in American History*. 14 vols. New York, 1913. Vol. 3.

Morison and Blum. *Letters of Theodore Roosevelt*. Vols. 1 and 2.

Roosevelt, Theodore. *An Autobiography*. New York, 1919.

Roosevelt Papers. Library of Congress. Washington, D.C.

Wisan, Joseph. *The Cuban Crisis as Reflected in the New York Press, 1895–1898*. New York, 1934.

Wolff, Leon. *Little Brown Brother*. London, 1961.

It was Mark Hanna who said (according to Beer, the source for Scene 7) that sending a warship on a friendly visit to Havana was "like waving a match in an oil well."

The sinking of the *Maine,* the proximate cause of the war, remains to this day a mysterious event. Although the navy's court of inquiry determined that the *Maine* had been destroyed by the detonation of a submarine mine, it refused to place responsibility for the explosion. (The U.S. would not allow Spain to participate in the inquiry, nor would it submit the matter to an international tribunal.) When the ship's remains were raised thirteen years later, a second court of inquiry upheld the general findings of the previous report. Historians have questioned the conclusiveness of both investigations, but a further examination is impossible, for what was left of the *Maine* was later sunk, with full military honors, at the bottom of the Gulf of Mexico.

The American public was quick to assume Spanish guilt. Senator Lodge summed up the nation's attitude when he said that it didn't matter whether or not the Spaniards had actually blown up the ship: they had created the conditions which led to the disaster. Headlines on the sinking are from Brown and contemporary newspaper accounts.

There is no single authoritative account of Roosevelt's famous afternoon as Acting Secretary of the Navy on February 25. The only one of Roosevelt's orders of that day to have been made public was the fateful command to Dewey (which Long let stand) to prepare offensive operations in the Pacific. In Scene 8, the additional orders dictated by Roosevelt are based on details in Long's *Journal* and Hagedorn's reconstruction. The confrontation between Long and TR is taken from the "Papers of John Davis Long," the *Journal,* Roosevelt's *Letters,* and the Roosevelt-Long correspondence in the Roosevelt manuscripts. Long's remark about being "overprepared for war" was made by Captain A. S. Crowninshield, Long's chief adviser, quoted in Garraty. Dewey's monologues are from his *Autobiography.* Roosevelt's aside about his usefulness in the Navy Department is from a letter in Morison, and his motto, "when in doubt," is from the *Autobiography*. Lodge made the tag comment many years later in his memorial addess to Congress after Roosevelt's death.

The actual influence of Roosevelt on the decision to attack the Spanish fleet in the Philippines is a matter of historical debate. Dewey believed that Roosevelt's order to him was the "first real step" toward active naval preparations for war; Roosevelt agreed that the order was of "much importance." In general, historians have accepted the notion that Dewey's victory at Manila — and the subsequent acquisition of the Philippines — would have been unlikely without Roosevelt's aggressive interference. Some, however, note that a plan for Pacific naval operations in the event of a war with Spain had been drawn up by naval strategists prior to Roosevelt's appointment.

Roosevelt's "chocolate éclair" and "white-livered cur" attacks against McKinley in Scene 9 are from Kohlsaat and Wolff. Lodge's anxious remarks about the fall elections come from letters to friends quoted in Garraty and in May.

The story of McKinley's meeting with Chicago *Tribune* publisher H. H. Kohlsaat in Scene 10 is related in *From McKinley to Harding*.

President McKinley did not actually deliver his war message in person. His address to Congress in Scene 11 combines background material on the Cuban situation from his annual message of December 6, 1897, with highlights of the special message he sent to Congress on April 11, 1898. Both are given in Miller. The description of the congressional reaction is from press reports in Bailey and Wisan, and an account in the Boston *Transcript*. The remark that the President "could have worked out the business without war" was made by Senator Spooner of Wisconsin and is quoted in Wolff.

The gossip of the clubmen in Scene 12 and senators in Scene 13 is quoted from letters of Lodge's friends Henry Lee Higginson and Winthrop Chanler and appears in Garraty.

FIGHTING THE SPANISH-AMERICAN WAR   ACT I: 14–19, 21–23

Blount, James H. *The American Occupation of the Philippines, 1898–1912*. New York, 1913.
Correspondence Relating to the War with Spain, April 15, 1898–July 30, 1902. 2 vols. Washington, 1902. Vol. 2.

Dewey. *Autobiography*.

Freidel, Frank. *The Splendid Little War*. Boston, 1958.

Harbaugh, William Henry. *Power and Responsibility: The Life and Times of Theodore Roosevelt*. New York, 1961.

Lodge. *Selections from the Roosevelt-Lodge Correspondence*. Vol. 1.

Morison and Blum. *Letters of Theodore Roosevelt*. Vol. 2.

Pettigrew, Richard. *Imperial Washington*. Chicago, 1922.

Roosevelt. *Autobiography*.

Before the war with Spain, the Regular U.S. Army, whose chief duty had been to protect the frontier and fight Indians, consisted of some twenty-six thousand men scattered across the country in small units. With the outbreak of war, many regular officers were commissioned in the state volunteer forces expressly authorized by Congress for the Cuban intervention. Roosevelt, with his special connections, was able to secure a position as lieutenant colonel of one of the three cavalry regiments organized by the federal government. He later became colonel of the regiment, but at the outset wisely deferred to the experience of army surgeon Leonard Wood (a Medal of Honor winner for his pursuit of Apache chief Geronimo), who headed the unit.

News that Roosevelt was organizing a cavalry regiment triggered thousands of applications from all over the country, although the unit was to be recruited mainly from the western territories. Roosevelt accepted some Ivy League graduates and New York policemen along with several hundred cowboys (and a few Indians). The meeting with Dean in Scene 14 gives some idea of the haphazard selection process going on across the nation. The conversation is adapted from Harbaugh.

Dewey's account of May 1 at Manila Bay in Scene 15 is from his *Autobiography*.

The Roosevelt-Lodge *Selections* is the source of the startlingly candid discussions of their "large policy" in Scenes 16–18, and of the Guam surrender in Scene 22. TR's description of Pettigrew is condensed from a quotation in *Imperial Washington*: "that particular swine seems to me, on the whole, the most obnoxious of the entire drove."

The source for Scene 19 (the singing of the Civil War ballad "The

Girl I Left Behind Me," the "great historical expedition," the sinking
sun over the Caribbean, and all) is a letter from Roosevelt to his
sister Corinne Robinson, which is given in Morison.

"We've got the Yankees on the run!" and "Don't cheer, men . . ."
in Scene 21 are famous quotations from the Spanish-American War
and may be found in Freidel.

The U.S. Consul at Manila wrote, as quoted in Blount, that the
Filipinos thronged about him after the May 1 victory, shouting "Viva
los Americanos!" We have reattributed the incident to Dewey himself. Dewey's statement that the Filipinos were "far superior" to the
Cubans may be found in the *Correspondence*. The Filipinos expected independence from the American intervention. One of Aguinaldo's early proclamations to his followers ran: "There, where you
see the American flag flying, assemble in numbers; they are our re-
deemers."

Scene 23 (TR in the trenches) combines letters from the *Selections*
with material from Roosevelt's *Autobiography*.

VICTORY   ACT I: 24, 25

Beveridge, Albert. *The Meaning of the Times*. Indianapolis, 1907.
Healy, Laurin Hall, and Lois Kutner. *The Admiral*. Chicago, 1944.
King, Moses. *The Dewey Reception*. New York, 1899.
Lodge. *Selections from the Roosevelt-Lodge Correspondence*. Vol.
1.
Shannon, David A., ed. *Progressivism and Postwar Disillusionment*,
1898–1928. New York, 1966.
Strong, Josiah. *Expansion Under New World Conditions*. New
York, 1900.
———. *The New Era*. New York, 1893.
———. *Our Country, It's Possible Future and Its Present Crisis*.
New York, 1891.
Thayer, William Roscoe. *The Life and Letters of John Hay*. 2
vols. Boston, 1915.
Wolff. *Little Brown Brother*.

In September, 1899, Commodore George Dewey returned home
from Manila. The greatest public celebration New York had ever
seen was given in his honor. All New York turned out, including

Tammany Boss Croker, whose exchange with Dewey is recorded in *The Admiral*. Other dialogue in Scene 24 is from *The Dewey Reception*, the New York *Journal*, and the *New York Times*. The remark "If I were a religious man . . ." is quoted by Wolff.

The real event suggested the stage event in this scene, a national self-apotheosis fed by diplomatic arrogance, business cupidity, military smugness, missionary zeal, and personal political ambitions. The speaker's address is from a much-quoted letter of John Hay to Roosevelt, in Thayer. The businessman's address is from a pamphlet of Postmaster General Charles Emory Smith, printed in Shannon. The general's speech is from an 1899 issue of *The Outlook* as quoted by Josiah Strong in *Expansion*. Strong was a midwestern Congregationalist minister whose popular books expressed the race-conscious spirit of evangelical expansionism in the last years of the century. The clergyman's address combines extracts from *Our Country* and *The New Era*. The wry Roosevelt remarks on politics are from letters to Lodge in the *Selections*. The Dewey ditty is in Wolff.

In Scene 25, Senator Beveridge's Indianapolis speech and the headlines which precede it are taken from home newspapers. Its final paragraph comes from his maiden speech to the Senate in January, 1900, a speech which enraged Senator Hoar because the words "Right, Justice, Duty, and Freedom" never once tempered his young colleague's enthusiasm for commercial opportunity in the Philippines. The speech is published in *The Meaning of the Times*.

MR. DOOLEY   ACT I: 20, 26

Dunne, Finley Peter. *Mr. Dooley in Peace and in War*. Boston, 1898.

Finley Peter Dunne's syndicated newspaper columns on the Spanish-American War brilliantly satirized U.S. military bungling and reflected the public's bewilderment over the sudden issue of "expansion." The columns, collected in *Mr. Dooley in Peace and in War*, the first and most successful of the series of Dooley books, were the source for the Dooley scenes in Act I.

THE ANTI-IMPERIALIST PROTEST   ACT II: 1, 26

Bancroft, Frederic, ed. *Speeches, Correspondence and Political Papers of Carl Schurz*. 6 vols. New York, 1913. Vol. 6.

Jordan, David Starr. *Imperial Democracy*. New York, 1899.

Lanzar, Maria Carpio. "The Anti-Imperialist League." *Philippine Social Science Review*, Vol. 3 (August, 1930).

The amount of anti-imperialist literature available is staggering. Letters, speeches, pamphlets, broadsides, meeting records, annual reports abound, and many of a very high literary quality, owing to the education and talents of the men involved in the movement.

One typical minor figure was David Starr Jordan, President of Leland Stanford University, a fragment of whose speech of February, 1899 ("red-handed in the very act"), we reattributed to chairman Boutwell at the opening of Act II. Apart from these three lines, the anti-imperialist meeting in Scene 1 consists of official business transacted and resolutions adopted at the meetings of June and November, 1898, and October, 1899, described in the CHRONOLOGY. Documents from the meetings appear in Bancroft and Lanzar.

The Schurz speeches in Scenes 1 and 26 are taken from his addresses dated January 4 and October 17, 1899, and September 28, 1900. The references to the election and third party are taken from his correspondence with anti-imperialists Charles Francis Adams and Edwin Burritt Smith, as quoted by Bancroft. The chant "Bring the boys home" is the merest reflection of the midwestern campaign to bring home the thousands of volunteer troops in the Philippines who had enlisted to fight Spain in the cause of humanity, but now felt it a "burning shame," as one of them put it, to fight the Filipinos.

ANDREW CARNEGIE'S CAMPAIGN   ACT II: 2, 3, 7
AGAINST THE TREATY

Carnegie, Andrew. "The Opportunity of the United States." *The North American Review*, Vol. 174 (May, 1902).

Carnegie Papers. Library of Congress.

Holt, William Stull. *Treaties Defeated by the Senate*. Boston, 1933.

Lodge. *Selections from the Roosevelt-Lodge Correspondence*. Vol. 1.

Millis, Walter. *The Martial Spirit*. Boston, 1931.

Thayer. *Life and Letters of John Hay*.

Tuchman, Barbara. *The Proud Tower*. New York, 1966.

Wolff. *Little Brown Brother*.

Carnegie may not have been "unsettled," as the *Herald* charged, but he was certainly distressed at the country's sudden grab for empire, and launched a frantic campaign to defeat the Treaty of Paris. His letter volumes at the Library of Congress, from which Scene 3 is drawn, suggest that he gave most of his time to the project between November, 1898, and the beginning of February, when the issue was decided. He exchanged letters on the subject with scores of anti-imperialists, among them Myrick and Atkinson, whose correspondence with Carnegie appears in this scene as dialogue. The letter to Secretary of State Hay combines three written in the course of a month (including the one about Scotch whisky). His astounding proposal to buy the Philippine Islands was rumored widely in the press, but not formally announced. Carnegie publicly confirmed that he was "perfectly serious" and "not bluffing" in his intention to purchase the archipelago. His press conference contains these and other verbatim published statements (the "insane root of territorial expansion" and "I would be glad indeed to see them shoot back"). His mordant joke ("I don't suppose they'd chase us . . .") is a reattribution from House Speaker Thomas Reed, as quoted in Wolff.

Hay obviously agreed with the editorial writer of the *Herald*. The denigrating material about Carnegie in Scene 7 is from a letter of Hay to New York *Tribune* publisher Whitelaw Reid, quoted in Thayer. McKinley's fatuous statement, "Carnegie doesn't understand the situation at all" was made at an interview with Carnegie before the outbreak of war, reported by Carnegie in *The North American Review*. His comment "we'll be the laughing stock of the world" was made to his secretary and is quoted in Millis. The pessimistic Lodge statements on the outcome of the Senate vote are from the *Selections*. Hay's remark ("A treaty of peace . . . ought to be ratified unaminously in twenty-four hours!") was adapted from a letter to Adams, quoted by Holt.

THE TREATY DEBATE   ACT II: 4–6, 8, 9

Bailey, Thomas A. "Was the Presidential Election of 1900 a Mandate on Imperialism?" *Mississippi Valley Historical Review*, Vol. 24 (June, 1937).

Carnegie, Andrew. *Autobiography of Andrew Carnegie.* New York, 1920.

Congressional Record, 55 Cong., 3 sess.; 56 Cong., 1 sess.
Dunn, Arthur W. *From Harrison to Harding*. 2 vols. New York, 1922. Vol. 1.
Lodge. *Selections from the Roosevelt-Lodge Correspondence*. Vol. 1.
Lodge Papers. Massachusetts Historical Society.
Miller. *Great Debates*. Vol. 3.
Morison and Blum. *Letters of Theodore Roosevelt*. Vol. 2.
Pettigrew, Richard. *Imperial Washington*.
——. *Triumphant Plutocracy*. New York, 1922.
Sheridan, Richard Brinsley. *The Filipino Martyrs*. London and New York, 1900.
Weinberg, Albert K. *Manifest Destiny*. Baltimore, 1935.

The Senate debate on the treaty was not actually transcribed, as it took place in executive session, Administration supporters claiming that national security would be breached by public discussion. However, a resolution introduced by Senator Vest of Missouri on the constitutionality of overseas colonial acquisition and other resolutions were heatedly debated in open session. The Senate discussions in Scenes 4, 6, and 9 are taken from debates on these resolutions scattered throughout the *Congressional Record* of January and February, 1899. (A shortened form of the debate appears in Volume 3 of Marion Miller's vast *Great Debates* collection, and makes thrilling reading.) In a few instances, the 1899 material was combined with portions of speeches delivered the following year when the question of retaining the Philippines came before the Senate.

The role of William Jennings Bryan in persuading wavering senators to support treaty ratification continues to be a subject of controversy. To Senator Hoar, Bryan's course was "as if some influential General in our Revolutionary War had surrendered West Point to the British," but others thought it convenient for Hoar, a party regular, to heap all the blame on Bryan. Historians are divided on the issue. William Stull Holt, for example, argues that Bryan's influence accounted for most of the non-Republican votes for the treaty. Paolo Coletta, on the other hand, absolves Bryan of ulterior motives in urging ratification and suggests that McKinley and Republican Senate leaders, with their promises of patronage, exerted far greater influence.

(See his article, "Bryan, McKinley and the Treaty of Paris," in the *Pacific Historical Review*, Vol. 26, of May, 1957.)

Views of participants on Bryan's actions are expressed in the invented encounter between Senators Allen and Pettigrew in Scene 8. Allen's lines defending Bryan appear in the *Congressional Record* of February 6, 1899. Pettigrew's material is based on his retrospective account of Bryan's intervention. A statement by a senator who does not appear in the play has been reattributed. Silver Republican Henry Teller's uneasy justification, "Suppose we do make a blunder." (from a *New York Times* interview), we have given to Allen. The quip "Byran would rather be wrong than be President," credited to Speaker Reed, is in Bailey. The newspaper report on the effect the fighting at Manila would have on the coming treaty vote appeared in the San Francisco *Call*, as quoted in Sheridan.

Carnegie's attack "one word from Mr. Bryan . . ." in Scene 9 is in his *Autobiography*. Bryan's line "Destiny is not as manifest as it was last week" is quoted by Weinberg.

Roosevelt's conversation with Lodge on the prospects of ratification in Scene 5 is from the *Selections*, the Roosevelt *Letters*, and material in the Lodge Papers at the Massachusetts Historical Society. Roosevelt's crude charge that Hoar was senile apparently so embarrassed Lodge that he omitted it from Roosevelt's February 7, 1899, letter in the *Selections*. The complete letter of that date appears in Morison.

PRESIDENT McKINLEY AND THE TAKING OF THE PHILIPPINES ACT II: 10

McKinley, William. *Speeches and Addresses of William McKinley, from March 1, 1897, to May 30, 1900.* New York, 1900.

Republican Party. *Republican Campaign Textbook, 1900.* Milwaukee, 1900.

After the Spanish-American War, McKinley toured the Midwest giving a series of equivocal speeches on Philippine annexation. At each stop, his staff carefully noted the level of applause on either side of the question. The warmer response to his pro-annexation statements apparently convinced the President to keep the archipelago.

Some scholars believe that McKinley had determined to take the islands from the first, but preferred to give an impression of reluctant acquiescence to popular demand. Certainly McKinley's actions after Dewey's victory indicated a consistent view about the desirability of American rule in the islands. Although the Filipinos expected independence and held control of most of the archipelago (except Manila, which they occupied jointly with American troops), McKinley ignored the establishment of Aguinaldo's government. Relations grew more strained when Filipinos were not allowed representation at the peace negotiations at Paris. The President's December, 1898, proclamation of "benevolent assimilation," warning the natives to accept the "strong arm of [American] authority," exacerbated tensions, although McKinley, unaware of the real situation, still hoped for a peaceful settlement. After the outbreak of hostilities, McKinley continued to follow an inflexible policy. He refused to negotiate with the rebels and demanded unconditional surrender. From his White House war room (according to the Boston *Herald*), he gave close attention to every detail of the campaign, carefully poring over troop movements and Otis' cables, frequently writing orders himself.

McKinley's speech in Scene 10 combines passages from a series of addresses he delivered defending his Philippine policy throughout the nation.

FIGHTING IN THE PHILIPPINES   ACT II: 11–25

Atkinson, Edward. *The Anti-Imperialist*. Boston, 1899–1900.
Bonsal, Stephen. *The Golden Horseshoe*. New York, 1900.
Correspondence Relating to the War with Spain. Vol. 2.
Olney, Warren. "The Clergy and the Conquest of the Philippines." *Oakland Enquirer*, April 25, 1899.
Storey, Moorfield, and M. P. Lichauco. *The Conquest of the Philippines by the United States, 1898–1925*. New York, 1926.
——, and Julian Codman. *Secretary Root's Record: Marked Severities in the Philippine Warfare*. Boston, 1902.
Wilcox, Marrion. *Harper's History of the War in the Philippines*. New York, 1900.
Wolff. *Little Brown Brother*.

Army songs aptly characterized the nature of the Philippine warfare. "If a lady wearin' pantaloons is swingin' wit' a knife" pointed to the insurgents' use of women soldiers. Other lyrics showed disenchantment with the prolonged fighting (Gen. Chaffee "Can occupy the Philippines with twenty thousand men/ . . . He quite forgot the date of this — the year two thousand ten"). "Damn, damn, damn the Filipinos" (which appears in Storey and Lichauco) was one of the army's most popular marching tunes. (The term "ladrone" means thief or bandit; "khakiak" refers to the Filipino's light brown skin color. "Krag" is the Krag-Jorgensen rifle in use at the time of the war.) The song was so offensive to natives that at one point, in a gesture to the friendly Filipinos, an American commanding officer banned its public singing. "Aguinaldo leads a sloppy life . . ." is quoted in Wolff.

In addition to the sources listed above, the war scenes rely heavily on our reading of contemporary newspapers and magazines. The press gave the war banner coverage in the first few months of fighting, but news from the front was harder to come by as guerrilla warfare deepened and the censorship became more stringent. Still, military coverage, editorial comment, special articles, and letters from soldiers appeared regularly. Many of the American correspondents at Manila (among them Albert G. Robinson of the New York *Evening Post*, John McCutcheon of the Chicago *Record*, John Bass of *Harper's Weekly* and the New York *Herald*, and Robert Collins of the Associated Press) wrote persistently, often brilliantly, of the military's attempt to fool the public about the progress of the war.

General Otis' cables to the War Department in the *Correspondence* are the source for his press interviews. The War Department, White House, and press tent scenes are taken from newspaper reports and *Harper's History*. Shafter's war plan to kill half the population is quoted in Olney.

Scene 18, on the early brutalities of the war (the burning, the shooting of prisoners), is based on soldiers' letters in *Marked Severities* and news reports in the *New York Times*, *Evening Post*, and *Harper's History*. Scene 25 is taken from soldiers' letters which appeared in these sources, and from letters in *The Anti-Imperialist* and *The Golden Horseshoe*.

The *Annual Reports of the War Department*, 1899–1902, the Philippine Information Society's pamphlets about the military campaign collected in *Facts About the Filipinos*, William Sexton's *Soldiers in the Sun,* and correspondent Robinson's *The Philippines: The War and the People* were useful reference sources for these scenes.

THEODORE ROOSEVELT'S NOMINATION   ACT II: 27, 28
TO THE VICE-PRESIDENCY

Beer. *Hanna.*
Davenport, Walter. *Power and Glory: The Life of Boies Penrose.*
New York, 1931.
Lodge. *Selections from the Roosevelt-Lodge Correspondence.*
Vol. 1.
McCaleb, Walter F. *Theodore Roosevelt.* New York, 1931.
Morison and Blum. *Letters of Theodore Roosevelt.* Vol. 2.

Theodore Roosevelt's account of his nomination to the vice-presidency, given in his *Autobiography* ("I . . . brought Senator Platt to terms"), differs from that of the party bosses. For their version, which we adopt, see Platt's *Autobiography* and the Davenport biography of Boies Penrose.

The meeting of the bosses in Scene 27 is based primarily on the account of Penrose, the junior Pennsylvania senator who was Quay's protégé, as described in Davenport. The meeting took place at the Walton Hotel in Philadelphia a few weeks before the Republican National Convention, and was attended by Senators Quay and Penrose, both anti-Hanna men, and Senator Platt of New York, who had come to win the support of the Pennsylvania bosses in ridding his state of Roosevelt. For dramatic purposes, we included Hanna in the meeting. Hanna's lines ("who will win your election for you") are quoted by Beer; his angry remark ("just one life between that crazy man and the presidency") is in McCaleb. The source for Platt's "Niagara Falls" comment is Morison.

Lodge wanted TR to seize the offer. For a good year they discussed the matter by mail between Albany and Washington, Roosevelt raising now one objection, now another. Until literally the last second, Lodge feared that Theodore would back out. Lodge was seated on the convention platform when TR stepped forward after being nominated. "You met me with a face of almost agonized anxiety," TR later gently teased his friend, "and put your head down on the table

191

as I began to speak." The source of their discussion in Scene 28 is the *Selections*.

THE ELECTION OF 1900   ACT II: 29-34

Correspondence Relating to the War with Spain. Vol. 2.
Dunne, Finley Peter. *Dissertations by Mr. Dooley.* New York, 1906.
——. "Mr. Dooley." *Harper's Weekly.* Vol. 44 (September 15, October 13, October 27, 1900).
——. *Mr. Dooley's Opinions.* New York, 1900.
Ellis, Elmer. *Mr. Dooley's America.* New York, 1941.
Foner, Philip. *Mark Twain, Social Critic.* New York, 1958.
Gibson, William. "Mark Twain and Howells: Anti-Imperialists." *New England Quarterly*, Vol. 20 (December, 1947).
Higginson, Thomas Wentworth. "George Frisbie Hoar." *Proceedings of the American Academy of Arts and Sciences*, Vol. 40 (July, 1904-July, 1905).
Morison and Blum. *Letters of Theodore Roosevelt.* Vol. 2.
Pettigrew. *Imperial Washington.*
——. *Triumphant Plutocracy.*
Philippine Information Society. *Facts About the Filipinos.* Boston, 1901.
Republican Party. *Official Proceedings of the Twelfth Republican National Convention.* Philadelphia, 1900.
Storey Papers. *Library of Congress.*

For anti-imperialists, the election of 1900 was the culmination of nearly two years of protest against "the President's war." After the collapse of the third-party movement, the defeat of imperialism at the polls focused on the candidacy of Bryan, whose credentials had been tarnished by his support for the Treaty of Paris. In addition, Bryan's radical economic policies (particularly the free coinage of silver), frightened away the more fiscally conservative anti-imperialists. The Democratic Party's brutal suppression of Negro rights in the South, in contrast to its championship of Filipino self-government, was also used effectively against Bryan. Shall we "strangle Booker Washington with one hand and wave the flag over the head of Aguinaldo with the other?" asked George Frisbie Hoar, who actively campaigned for the Republican ticket. Most anti-imperialists went reluctantly for Bryan ("It is a choice between evils and I am going to shut my eyes, hold my nose, vote, go home, and disinfect myself," wrote former Secretary of Agriculture J. S. Morton to ex-President Cleveland), but some supported him wholeheartedly. William James of Harvard, a leading anti-imperialist, said he would vote for Bryan "with both hands."

The convention speech (" 'Teddy' was the child of Fifth Avenue") comes from the nominating speech of New York Senator Chauncey Depew, in the *Official Proceedings* of the Republican convention. Roosevelt's line "The thing could not be helped" is from a letter to his sister Anna Cowles, in Morison. Mr. Dooley's campaign reflections are from *Mr. Dooley's Opinions*, the *Dissertations*, *Mr. Dooley's America*, and *Harper's Weekly*. Mr. Twain was met by reporters after a long exile in Europe. The interviews appeared in the New York *Tribune* (quoted in Gibson) and the *New York Times*. Foner is the source for the "Anti-Doughnut Party."

The account of the third-party demise in Scene 32 is taken from Pettigrew. His remark about Hoar is a reattribution from Massachusetts anti-imperialist Thomas Wentworth Higginson. (Higginson was commenting on Hoar's "right-about-face" on Panama, but the charge is typical of many made against Hoar on the Philippine issue. Lodge and Hay, according to Henry Adams, were "struck dumb" to find Hoar, on the morning after the treaty vote, "sitting by the President's side, with arms about his neck as it were, unctuous, affectionate, beaming . . . slobbering the President with assurances of his admiration.")

The failure of the election to end Filipino resistance resulted in escalation of American military action. The anonymous officer's admission in Scene 34 that the "American army is on the defensive" was reported after the election in the New York *Evening Post*. (The report is one of several hundred clippings in the Moorfield Storey scrapbooks at the Library of Congress, an excellent source on the Philippine War.) The fragments about MacArthur's failed election prediction are from the *Correspondence*; the fragment on dual government is from a report by John McCutcheon reprinted in *Facts About the Filipinos*.

Aptheker, Herbert. *A Documentary History of the Negro People in the United States.* New York, 1951.
Flower, B. O. "Some Dead Sea Fruit of Our War of Subjugation." *The Arena*, Vol. 27 (June, 1902).
Ministers' Meeting of Protest Against the Atrocities in the Philippines. Boston, 1902.
The Nation, Vol. 74 (May 1, 1902).
Senate Document 331, 57 Cong., 1 sess. *Affairs in the Philippine Islands,* Hearings before the Committee on the Philippines of the United States Senate. 3 vols. Washington, 1902. Vols. 2 and 3.
Storey and Codman. *Marked Severities in the Philippine Warfare.*
Welsh, Herbert. *By Way of Manila.* Philadelphia, 1902.
———. *To Lincoln's Plain People.* Philadelphia, 1903.

The capture of Aguinaldo in the spring of 1901 was expected to end the war once and for all, but active revolt continued throughout the year in several important areas. In September, natives of Balangiga, on the island of Samar, attacked the U.S. garrison, whose protection had been requested by the village mayor, thought to be loyal to the U.S. Most of the American soldiers, surprised at their breakfast, were brutally slaughtered with native bolos. To quell the disturbances in Samar, the commanding officer, Brigadier General Jacob Smith, initiated a rigorous policy of action against the Filipinos, including the reconcentration of noncombatants and other drastic measures. In the unpacified area of Batangas, south of Manila, the new military governor, Brigadier General James Bell, issued a series of written orders providing for extreme measures against the civilian population. The rigid pacification policies of Bell and Smith appeared to be the result of the replacement of General MacArthur with General Adna Chaffee. Chaffee had a reputation for harsh methods, gained in the allied expedition he led against the Boxers in Peking.

The generals' orders are based primarily on General Bell's circulars to his station commanders, printed in the 1902 Senate *Hearings*. Smith's verbal orders were widely quoted in newspaper stories of his court-martial, and appear in the court-martial records. Chaffee's remarks combine material of Chaffee and Bell, from the *Hearings*. His comment on a people "absolutely hostile to the white race" was quoted in a *Nation* article of May, 1902.

Stories of widespread army cruelties against Filipino natives were reported by soldiers at the Senate hearings. O'Brien's account of the La Nog massacre, Flint's description of water torture, and Smith's story come from this source. The country was soon flooded with reports of atrocities. *The Arena* published an article describing a variety of tortures including "progressive wounding," from which the account in this scene is taken. Philadelphia publisher Herbert Welsh printed many news reports and letters on the atrocities in his weekly, *City and State*. The Howze whippings, Miller's torture story, and the bridge massacre come from pamphlets reprinted in this paper. The anti-imperialists, who believed the hearings had been a whitewash, set up an investigating committee which published its own review of army conduct, *Marked Severities*. The report of the hanging torture is taken from this work. The private's account of the water cure ("sometimes kerosene or coconut oil are used") come from a denunciation of the atrocities at the Boston ministers' protest meeting. The Weir atrocity report comes from the Boston *Transcript*.

Many Americans believed that racism influenced the army's brutal policies against the Filipinos. ("If there ever was a war of races in this world, the war in the Philippines is precisely that," wrote anti-imperialists Boutwell, Higginson, and William Lloyd Garrison, Jr., all of them associated with the abolitionist movement, in an open letter to black Americans.) The statement of Major Gardener that "the natives are beginning to understand what 'nigger' means" was made in a report to Governor General Taft charging extensive army cruelties. The report, printed as a *Hearings* exhibit, became a major issue despite the efforts of the War Department and Senate Republicans to discredit it. The black soldier's speech is taken from a letter to the Indianapolis *Freeman*, quoted in Aptheker. The soldier was serving in one of four black regiments in the Philippines. It was our invention to place him with the Ninth Cavalry and have him report the desertion of his comrades. The line on the black deserters is from a *New York Times* article reporting the execution of two Ninth Cavalry soldiers in February, 1902. They were tried by a military court after their capture, President Roosevelt personally declining to interfere with the sentence. (There is documentation that nearly a dozen white soldiers sympathetic to the Filipino cause also deserted. However, we came across no evidence that any of these soldiers was executed.)

THE LOPEZ FAMILY

ACT III: 2

Senate Document 331. Hearings on *Affairs in the Philippine Islands*. Vol. 3.

The remarkable correspondence of the Lopez brothers and sisters was gathered into a book by their anti-imperialist American friends, and eventually found its way into the Senate's 1902 hearings as an exhibit. The wealthy, landowning Batangas family initially had mixed attitudes toward the American occupation. At one extreme were Cipriano, an insurgent officer, and Sixto, a prominent Filipino nationalist who published many pro-Aguinaldo articles in the United States; at the other, Mariano, who actively cooperated with American authorities. The brave journey of Clemencia to the United States to plead for her imprisoned brothers ended unsuccessfully, although she made many devoted friends among anti-imperialists during her stay. Scene 2 combines letters of two younger sisters, Juliana and Maria.

PROTESTS AGAINST THE ATROCITIES

ACT III: 3–5

Beveridge. *The Meaning of the Times*.
Congressional Record, 56 Cong., 1 sess.; 57 Cong., 1 sess.; 57 Cong., 2 sess.
Mass Meetings of Protest Against the Suppression of the Truth About the Philippines. Boston, 1903.
Ministers' Meeting of Protest.
Senate Document 166, 57 Cong., 1 sess. *Anti-Imperialist Petition Requesting Investigation of Army Practices*, 1902.
Welsh, Herbert. *"Fiat Lux": The Suppression of Truth*. Boston, 1903.

Protest against the atrocities was joined by citizens of both parties in all walks of life, many of them previously unassociated with the anti-imperialist movement. Hundreds of citizens, including many prominent university professors, signed petitions to Congress demanding an investigation of army conduct. In Boston, clergymen of all faiths met at Tremont Temple to present a "united front against barbarity" and to urge the President to punish the wrongdoers. In the Senate, the issue became the subject of a violent partisan debate, with Democrats charging army cruelty and Republicans defending military honor. Eight months after the war's official conclusion, anti-imperialists in Boston organized "mass meetings of protest" against the "suppression of truth" by President Roosevelt and Senator Lodge (who refused to reopen his committee's hearings). Storey's speech in Scene 3 is from his address on that occasion. The Senate discussion in Scene 4 is based on the debate of spring, 1902. The final passage of Hoar's speech is taken from his famous April, 1900, "Lust of Empire" address. Carmack's speech includes two passages ("you might as well write a letter to a dead man"; and "Not to avoid guilt, sir, only to avoid shame") from speeches in the winter of 1903. Beveridge's remarks on Cuba and on the "barnacles" may be found in speeches of this period in the *Meaning of the Times*. The Montclair Mass in Scene 5 was reported in the New York *Tribune*.

THE ASSASSINATION OF McKINLEY ACT III: 6, 7

Kohlsaat. *From McKinley to Harding*.
Olcott, Charles S. *The Life of William McKinley*. 2 vols. Boston, 1916. Vol. 2.

McKinley confided his reasons for taking the Philippines to a group of Methodist ministers visiting the White House in November, 1899. A report of the interview by one of those present, General James F. Rusling, appeared in *The Christian Advocate* some years later and was reprinted by Charles Olcott in his *Life of McKinley*. Although Olcott wrote that Rusling's account was confirmed by others present, some historians have questioned its authenticity because Rusling apparently presented a similar report of a meeting with Lincoln after the battle of Gettysburg.

"White House Blues" is one of many versions of a popular folk song, known also as "Mister McKinley" and "Zolgotz," after McKinley's Polish assassin. Hanna's remark on "that goddamned cowboy" was made to Kohlsaat aboard the funeral train carrying McKinley, and is reported in *From McKinley to Harding*.

For dramatic effect, McKinley's assassination occurs in the play after the peak of protest against war atrocities. McKinley died in September, 1901, a few months before the general public learned of the army brutalities, many of which nonetheless occurred during his Administration.

HEARINGS ACT III: 8

Blount. *American Occupation of the Philippines*.
Senate Document 331. Hearings on *Affairs in the Philippine Islands*. Vols. 1 and 2.

When the conduct of the army became a major political issue in early 1902, the Senate Committee on the Philippines, chaired by Henry Cabot Lodge, reluctantly agreed to hold hearings. Lodge played a minor role during the hearings, leaving the chief work of defending the Administration's Philippine policy to Beveridge.

The hearings, which were held in closed session, lasted nearly five months and produced three thousand pages of testimony. The Republicans called to the stand officials who had played a major role in suppressing the rebellion — among them Generals MacArthur and Hughes and Governor General Taft, all of whom praised the humane conduct of the American forces. More sensational was the surprise testimony of a dozen soldiers (most were brought to the attention of the committee's Democratic minority by anti-imperialists) who revealed the army's extensive practices of torture, reconcentration, the burning of barrios, and the killing of prisoners in cold blood. Republican senators stifled the attempt of the opposition to summon additional witnesses, including Aguinaldo, Edward Atkinson of Boston, and Major Gardener, the army officer whose written report condemned military brutality and racism.

Scene 8 is taken from the hearings. One passage of Taft's speech (". . . Mafia on a very large scale") is taken from an earlier report of Taft to the War Department, quoted in Blount. The line "They burn them alive and throw them into wells" is taken from an interview with Funston reported in the New York *Tribune*.

Flower, B. O. "Some Dead Sea-Fruit of Our War of Subjugation."
Roosevelt Papers. Library of Congress.
Senate Document 213. 57 Cong., 2 sess. *Trials of Courts-Martial
in the Philippine Islands in Consequence of Certain Instructions.*
Washington, 1903.
Senate Document 331. Hearings on *Affairs in the Philippine Is-
lands.* Vol. 2.

The President's decision to court-martial General Smith and others
alleged to have committed outrages against natives was hailed
throughout the country, although many agreed with the *Arena* writer
who believed Roosevelt acted somewhat tardily. Six officers were
eventually brought to trial under his order. The *Arena* article, and the
instructions to General Chaffee ordering court-martials, a *Hearings* exhibit, are the source for the reporter's remarks at the opening of Scene
9. The court-martial dialogue is taken from the trial proceedings,
printed in *Sen. Doc.* 213. The report of the President's review of the
Smith court-martial and the army officer's comment that he was
making a "political example" of Smith in Scene 10 appear in a *New
York Times* clipping in the Roosevelt scrapbooks at the Library of
Congress.

Although the President and Secretary of War disapproved of
Smith's "exceptional" command to "kill and burn," they expressly
sanctioned the written orders of Chaffee, Bell, and Smith as justified
by the treacherous nature of the enemy. Both maintained that the
policies of retaliation and reconcentration were in strict conformity
with the nation's code of military conduct. The anti-imperialists'
demand for a new investigation, submitted to Roosevelt along with
evidence of additional atrocities, was abruptly dismissed.

THE END OF THE WAR   ACT III: 11, 12

Adams. *The Education of Henry Adams.*
Bancroft. *Schurz Papers.* Vol. 6.
Meyer Papers. Massachusetts Historical Society.
Morison and Blum. *Letters of Theodore Roosevelt.* Vol. 2.

Roosevelt, Theodore. *Presidential Addresses and State Papers.* 10
vols. New York, 1910. Vol. 1.

Roosevelt Papers. Library of Congress.

Root Papers. Library of Congress.

Sexton, William Thaddeus. *Soldiers in the Sun: An Adventure in
Imperialism.* Harrisburg, Pa., 1939.

The afternoon at Sagamore Hill is an invention based on letters in
manuscript collections and other sources. Root's prediction ("a matter of merely historical interest") and comments on the nation's
political mood are from his letters of October 4, 1902, to Connecticut
Senator Orville Platt and other friends. Lodge's ("I doubt it will be
mentioned in the next campaign") is adapted from a May, 1903, letter to George Meyer. Roosevelt's statement "we haven't a single incident in the Philippines as bad as the massacre at Wounded Knee"
is from the draft of an extraordinary letter to Commanding General
Nelson A. Miles in the Roosevelt Papers. (Roosevelt was uncomfortable in having Miles, an anti-imperialist sympathizer, as the army's
top officer. His angry letter was in response to an end-the-war plan
Miles proposed, and to his allegations of military brutality in the Philippines. When Roosevelt refused to authorize the plan, Miles made
his charges public. Roosevelt wanted to remove the "blackguard and
scoundrel," but Miles' great popularity ensured his position. The
substance of Roosevelt's letter to Miles is in one to Root on February
18, 1902, which appears in Morison.)

Other material in this scene is based on Adams' characterization of
TR ("pure Act"); a Schurz letter to Carnegie denouncing the court-
martial punishments as "almost farcical"; and Roosevelt's letter to
Schurz (one of many attacking him), calling him "a dog."

In spite of the official termination of the Philippine War, guerrilla
fighting — especially severe in the southern islands — continued
sporadically for several years. In 1903, the policy of reconcentration
was pursued in Samar, Albay, Cavite, and Tayabas. Accounts of
reconcentration in Batangas were still being reported two years later.
In 1906, the slaughter of six hundred Moro men, women, and children gathered in a crater near mount Dajo caused President Roosevelt
to congratulate the army on its "brilliant feat of arms." The incident,
however, received little editorial comment. (Appalled at the lack of

public response, Mark Twain wrote a searing essay on the massacre.)

With the public swiftly losing interest in Philippine affairs, and with profits from the Philippine trade insubstantial, even imperialists became disillusioned. Concerned about public apathy and the islands' strategic vulnerability, Roosevelt wrote to Secretary of War Taft in 1907 that the Philippines were our "heel of Achilles." The anti-imperialists, however, though few in number, continued the fight against colonialism until the disintegration of their league more than a decade later. The Philippines received independence in 1946.

SELECTED BIBLIOGRAPHY
OF SECONDARY WORKS

Agoncillo, Teodoro A. *Malolos, the Crisis of the Republic.* Quezon City, 1960.
One of the few studies of the Philippine Revolution and Aguinaldo's government.

Alfonso, Oscar M. *Theodore Roosevelt and the Philippines, 1897–1909.* Quezon City, 1970.
An examination of Roosevelt's role in the formulation of Philippine policy.

Beisner, Robert L. *Twelve Against Empire: The Anti-Imperialists, 1898–1900.* New York, 1968.
A view of prominent Mugwump and "out of step" Republican anti-imperialists as conservative and nostalgically idealistic.

Gates, John Morgan. *Schoolbooks and Krags: The United States Army in the Philippines, 1898–1902.* Westport, Ct., 1973.
Argues that the army's program in the Philippines was characterized by benevolence and humanitarian reform.

Grenville, John A. S., and George Berkeley Young. *Politics, Strategy and American Diplomacy.* New Haven, 1966. Chaps. 8, 9, 10.
A revisionist interpretation of the "large policy," McKinley's leadership, and the acquisition of the Philippines.

May, Ernest R. *American Imperialism: A Speculative Essay.* New York, 1968.
Provides a synthesis of other theories, and a tentative new explanation of the grab for empire after the Spanish-American War.

Millis, Walter. *The Martial Spirit.* Boston, 1931.
Still the best popular account of the war with Spain.

Schirmer, Daniel B. *Republic or Empire: American Resistance to the Philippine War.* Cambridge, 1972.

A revealing and sympathetic study of the Boston anti-imperialists from a New Left point of view.

Sexton, William Thaddeus. *Soldiers in the Sun: An Adventure in Imperialism.* Harrisburg, Pa., 1939.

A military history of the war by a U.S. army captain who served in the Philippines in the 1930s.

Tompkins, E. Berkeley. *Anti-Imperialism in the United States: The Great Debate, 1890–1920.* Philadelphia, 1970.

A comprehensive history of the movement with an extensive bibliography on anti-imperialism.

Wolff, Leon. *Little Brown Brother.* London, 1961.

The best overall account of the Philippine War.

BIOGRAPHIES

ADAMS, HENRY BROOKS (1838–1918), historian, biographer, novelists, great-grandson of one President of the United States and grandson of another. He began his own distinguished career teaching medieval history at Harvard and editing *The North American Review*. Settling later in Washington, his close ties with the capital's inner Republican circle (the Roosevelts, Lodges, Hays, and others) led him to write of himself, "So far as he had a function in life, it was as stable-companion to statesmen." *The Education of Henry Adams* is his best-known work.

ALLEN, WILLIAM VINCENT (1847–1924), elected to the U.S. Senate from Nebraska as a Populist in 1893. Widely respected beyond third-party circles, Allen was known as the "intellectual giant of Populism." In 1896, as chairman of the Populist presidential nominating convention, he supported the Democratic-Populist standard bearer, William Jennings Bryan, who championed the cause of free silver to which Allen was dedicated. He was defeated for reelection in 1899, but served in the Senate until 1901 in the place of his successor-elect, who died before taking office.

ATKINSON, EDWARD (1827–1905), Boston manufacturer, founder of a fire insurance company, economist, statistician, dietitian, inventor, Mugwump reformer. Among his many interests was the improvement of laborers' working and living conditions. His "Aladdin's oven" permitted the slow cooking of meat at controlled temperatures, resulting in reduced food and fuel costs for workers. Labor leaders were highly critical of "Shinbone Atkinson" and his cheap diets, fearing that lowered living costs would force down wages. Later Atkinson became one of the most militant (and prolific) of anti-expansionists, serving as vice-president and unofficial statistician of the Anti-Imperialist League. He published *The Anti-Imperialist*, a lively journal of documents, soldiers' letters, and Atkinson's antiwar articles. The pamphlets became a cause célèbre when two issues en route to the Philippines were confiscated by the government for their "seditious" content. Even former admirers denounced Atkinson as a traitor for encouraging American soldiers to refuse to enlist or fight in "unlawful service" in the Philippines. The incident spurred great interest in the pamphlets and the triumphant author eventually distributed over one hundred thousand of them within the U.S.

BACON, AUGUSTUS OCTAVIUS (1839–1914), Democratic senator from Georgia, elected first in 1894, and for the fourth time in 1913, when he became, under the 17th Amendment, the first directly elected U.S. senator. Bacon was ranking Democrat on the committees on Rules, the Judiciary, and Foreign Relations (of which he became chairman in 1913). Although not a towering figure in the public eye, Bacon was an influential and respected Senate leader, expert in constitutional questions and foreign affairs. According to a colleague, Bacon was a "connecting link" between the old and the new South — dignified, aristocratic, and gentle, but imbued with the progressive spirit and aspirations of modern America.

BELL, JAMES FRANKLIN (1856–1919), a seasoned Indian fighter, who earned the Congressional Medal of Honor and appointment as a brigadier general under MacArthur in the Philippines. He commanded a regiment known as the "suicide club," which conducted the most difficult part of MacArthur's campaign into the interior of northwestern Luzon in 1899. In 1901 Bell became brigade commander for Southern Luzon, where he relentlessly pacified the holdout province of Batangas. He was called the "American Weyler" after the notorious Spanish commandante "Butcher" Weyler, who brutally put down the insurrection in Cuba. President Roosevelt appointed him Chief of Staff in 1906.

BEVERIDGE, ALBERT JEREMIAH (1862–1927), U.S. senator, Progressive leader, historian, biographer. His extraordinary oratorical ability brought Beveridge, then a young attorney, to the attention of the Indiana State Legislature, which elected him to the U.S. Senate in 1899. His maiden speech on the Philippines ("'Twas a speech ye cud waltz to," said Mr. Dooley) made him a national figure. A strong nationalist like Theodore Roosevelt, Beveridge advocated positive government action at home and abroad: he was a leader of the Progressive movement (especially active in the campaign against child labor) and a zealous champion of imperialism. He was defeated after two terms because of his role in the Progressive insurgency against old guard Republican forces. Successive attempts at reelection, both as a Progressive and a Republican, failed. Beveridge was a respected historical writer, best known for his four-volume biography of U.S. Chief Justice John Marshall. He died with a biography of Lincoln in progress.

BOUTWELL, GEORGE SEWALL (1818–1905), Massachusetts governor before the Civil War, commissioner of the new Department of Internal Revenue under Lincoln, and later, successively, U.S. congressman, Secretary of the Treasury, and U.S. senator. Like so many of the New England anti-imperialists, Boutwell began his political career as an abolitionist. After the Civil War, then a leading Radical Republican in Congress, he was prominent in the movement to impeach President Johnson. Boutwell played an important role in Republican affairs until he left the Party over the Philippine question, supporting Bryan in the 1900 election. He was president of the New England Anti-Imperialist League from its formation in November, 1898, to his death, as well as president of the national anti-imperialist organization.

CARMACK, EDWARD WARD (1858–1908), Tennessee Democrat, elected to the U.S. Senate in 1901 after a career as a crusading newspaper editor and two-term congressman. Among Carmack's causes were prohibition, good government, and white supremacy. One black newspaper, the Cleveland *Gazette*, called him "a very Saul in his persecution of the Negro." Carmack was opposition leader of the Senate's Committee on the Philippines. During its 1902 hearings, his scalding wit caused much discomfort to Administration senators attempting to put the best possible face on army conduct in the Philippines. In 1906 he was defeated for governor of Tennessee on a prohibition platform. Anti-prohibition followers of his opponent killed him two years later in a Nashville street brawl.

CARNEGIE, ANDREW (1835–1919), industrialist and philanthropist, a Scottish emigrant at the age of 13, who started as a cotton factory bobbin boy, advanced to messenger in a Pittsburgh telegraph office, and ended as a steel millionaire. Carnegie was an idealistic believer in the republican institutions of his adopted country. Carnegie served the Anti-Imperialist League as chief financial supporter and vice-president. He was inexhaustible (if sometimes contradictory) in his efforts against imperialism. In later life Carnegie preached the "gospel of wealth" (the title of his famous essay), and practiced it through unprecedented public gifts to education, peace, scientific research, and the extension of the public library system.

CHAFFEE, ADNA ROMANZA (1842–1914), Civil War veteran and Southwest Indian fighter, who rose rapidly in the army after distinguished service at El Caney in Cuba. Promoted to colonel in the regular army, Chaffee was selected to head the allied relief expedition to Peking after the Boxer outbreak. His reputation there as an aggressive disciplinarian led to his appointment in 1901 as commanding general in the Philippines, with the rank of major general. In 1904, he became Chief of Staff, serving until his retirement two years later.

CROKER, RICHARD (1841–1922), New York City politician, the son of Irish immigrants, who spent his boyhood as a gang leader and prizefighter. He was charged with the election-day murder in 1874 of a member of a rival political faction, but the case was dismissed for lack of evidence. He later admitted that one of his men had commited the murder in self-defense. Allied with the anti-Tweed "Young Democracy" division of Tammany Hall, Croker held a string of political patronage offices before becoming Tammany chief in 1886. He ruled New York City through his absolute mastery of the spoils system. Croker accumulated a fortune by the end of his career through what a colleague called "honest graft." After the decline of his political power, he bred racing horses in England.

DEWEY, GEORGE (1837–1917), Civil War naval veteran, favored by Navy Assistant Secretary Theodore Roosevelt for command of the Asiatic Squadron when that post fell vacant in 1897. ("I knew that in the event of war, Dewey could be slipped like a wolfhound from a leash.") Roosevelt prodded Dewey to use political influence to secure his appointment, and Senator Proctor of Vermont, Dewey's home state, was obliging. After his brilliant victory at Manila, Dewey returned home in triumph. New York City built an arch for his parade; the American people gave him a house in Washington; Congress created a new rank for him, Admiral of the Navy. In 1900, Dewey engaged in a naive flirtation with presidential politics (some blamed his ambitious new wife) and abruptly fell from public favor. Thereafter he served with distinction as president of the General Board of the Navy, playing a leading role in the formulation of national defense policy.

DOOLEY, MR. MARTIN, fictional Irish saloonkeeper created by Finley Peter Dunne (1867–1936), humorist and journalist. In 1893, Dunne began a series of columns in a Chicago paper setting down the "conversations" of Mr. Dooley and his various Irish cronies of the "Sixth Wa-ard." Mr. Dooley soared to fame in 1898 through Dunne's hilarious pieces on the Spanish-American War. The columns, nationally syndicated, dialect and all, had an extraordinary influence. They were quoted regularly at cabinet meetings. Mr. Dooley commented on many phases of American social life — the woman question, law, marriage, sports. He was especially devastating on war, politics, and racial justice ("Take up th' white man's burden, an' hand it to th' coon"). The Dooley columns appeared intermittently through 1915. Many were published in slim volumes that remain popular to this day.

FORAKER, JOSEPH BENSON (1846–1917), successful corporation lawyer, Ohio governor, later elected to the U.S. Senate in 1896 and 1902. This combative debater ("Fire Alarm Joe") was one of the Administration's chief constitutional lawyers. The conservative senator frequently clashed with President Roosevelt. The final break came when Foraker led the opposition to Roosevelt's abrupt dismissal of an entire Negro regiment for alleged participation in a riot at

Brownsville, Texas. He unsuccessfully challenged President Taft in 1908 for the Republican presidential nomination. Muckraking charges that Foraker was the "representative of the interests" were borne out with the disclosure that he received fees from Standard Oil while in the Senate. The revelation forced his retirement in 1909. In 1914 he was defeated by Warren G. Harding in Ohio's senatorial primary.

FUNSTON, FREDERICK (1865–1917), military hero and adventurer best known for his daring capture of Filipino rebel leader Emilio Aguinaldo. He began his military career fighting Spaniards in the Cuban insurgent army in 1896. After the outbreak of the Spanish-American War, Funston was given command of the 20th Kansas Regiment in the U.S. Volunteer Cavalry, and sent to the Philippines. His orders to "take no prisoners" at Calumpit in February, 1899, made him a particular object of anti-imperialist attacks. He was awarded the Medal of Honor for his bravery in this battle. Two years later anti-imperialists denounced his use of bribery, forgery, and native mercenaries in the capture of Aguinaldo. For this exploit, he was promoted to brigadier general in the regular army. In 1902 Funston was reprimanded by President Roosevelt for his intemperate public talks defending army conduct in the Philippines and attacking Senator Hoar's "overheated conscience" and "peanut politics." Funston served in Cuba, Hawaii, and again in the Philippines before his promotion to major general in 1914, when he led the expedition to Vera Cruz during the American intervention in Mexico.

GARDENER, CORNELIUS (1849–1921), West Point graduate with a distinguished thirty-year career in army service, whose criticism of army conduct in the Philippines resulted in his "persecution" (according to the Boston *Herald*) by the "whole military machine." In March, 1901, Gardener became governor of Tayabas in Luzon, considered a pacified province. His charge that the army's systematic cruelties were "sowing the seeds for a perpetual revolution" was made in his annual report to Governor General Taft. The War Department withheld the report from the Senate's Philippine Committee. It attracted national attention when Democratic committee members (with the probable help of the army's anti-imperialist Commanding General Nelson Miles) revealed the suppression. Gardener's disclosures brought angry denials from the War Department, which blocked his appearance as a witness before the Senate hearings.

HANNA, MARCUS ALONZO (1837–1904), millionaire Cleveland industrialist and shrewd political manager who became a President-maker by promoting the candidacy of Ohio governor William Mc-Kinley. He was McKinley's closest adviser. To find room for Hanna in the Senate, McKinley appointed Ohio's feeble Senator John Sherman Secretary of State, although Sherman's near senility was an open secret in Washington. Then the Ohio governor, under strong White House pressure, appointed Hanna to fill Sherman's unexpired term. Hanna narrowly won election to the Senate seat. Charges that the victory was gained through bribery were later dismissed by a Senate investigating committee. Hanna is considered the first modern polit-ical manager in history. He was chairman of the Republican National Committee in 1896 and 1900, collecting huge contributions through unprecedented assessments on businesses. Hanna was the nation's leading advocate of strong government action in support of business interests. Popular cartoons depicted him as a plutocrat covered with dollar signs. However, some business leaders considered his doctrine of the "harmony of interests" between capital and labor too liberal. Hanna was reelected to the Senate in 1903, but died the following winter.

HAY, JOHN MILTON (1838–1905), Secretary of State under Mc-Kinley and Roosevelt, historian, poet, novelist. His brilliant career had humble origins in his uncle's law offices in Springfield, Illinois. The lawyer next door was Abraham Lincoln, who brought young Hay to the White House as his private secretary. Hay had an extensive diplomatic career in the 1860s. In the next decades he became one of America's leading literary figures, the author of popular volumes of poetry, a best-selling anti-labor novel, *The Bread-Winners*, and a mon-umental ten-volume study of Abraham Lincoln, written with John Nicolay. Hay's excoriating wit and suavity adorned the Washington circle of gentlemen-statesmen gathered about his intimate friend Henry Adams. The two friends observed the capital scene from neighboring town houses on Lafayette Square, opposite the White

House. Hay returned to public life in 1897 as McKinley's ambassador to Great Britain, becoming Secretary of State the following year. His "Open Door" policy in China established Hay as a brilliant statesman and became a cornerstone of American diplomacy. In later years it was criticized as ineffectual and naive.

HOAR, GEORGE FRISBIE (1826–1904), Massachusetts Republican of a distinguished Concord family, who served four House and five Senate terms. He was the grandson of Roger Sherman, a signer of the Declaration of Independence and the Constitution, and the son of Samuel Hoar, the chairman of the convention that launched Massachusetts' Free Soil Party. The younger Hoar was also active in anti-slavery politics, becoming a charter member of the Massachusetts Republican Party. Hoar's participation in the abolitionist crusade left him with a continuing commitment to racial justice. Along with other anti-imperialist leaders, he saw the Philippine adventure in racial terms. He entered Congress as a Radical Republican after the Civil War, and later acceded to the Senate seat of his hero, the abolitionist Charles Sumner. Hoar was chairman of the Judiciary Committee and widely respected as the "dean" of the Senate, although reformers sometimes accused him of excessive party regularity. He was the reluctant ally of Democratic, and especially Mugwump, anti-imperialists, despising these long-standing political foes almost as much — or more — than imperialism. Younger Republicans of the progressive stripe regarded Hoar's interest in individual rights and his faith in moral suasion as a relic of a bygone political period. The *New York Times* denounced his program of civil rights, women's suffrage, and universal education as "socialistic mush." From a modern perspective Hoar seems more farsighted than many of his contemporaries.

HUGHES, ROBERT P. (1839–1909), career army officer who began his military service with the Union forces in the Civil War. Hughes was sent to the Philippines in 1898, becoming a brigadier general and chief of staff of the Eighth Corps. He was later assigned to head the Department of the Visayas, which included the rebellious Province of Samar under the local command of General "Hell-Roaring Jake" Smith.

KOHLSAAT, HERMAN HENRY (1853–1924), a self-made man of immigrant parents who earned a fortune from a wholesale bakery and chain of Chicago luncheonettes. His activities in the Republican party in Illinois led to his friendship with William McKinley, whose congressional advocacy of the protective tariff he admired. In 1893, with Mark Hanna and others, he helped to rescue McKinley, then Ohio governor, from personal bankruptcy. In 1895, Kohlsaat became editor-publisher of the Chicago *Times-Herald,* and put its influence behind the gold standard and other Republican policies. In his entertaining memoir, *From McKinley to Harding,* Kohlsaat describes himself as a friend and adviser to five U.S. Presidents.

LODGE, HENRY CABOT (1850–1924), U.S. senator from Massachusetts, scion of a prominent New England merchant family, the "scholar in politics" who became a historian at the urging of his Harvard professor Henry Adams but soon abandoned his own Harvard teaching post for a political career. Lodge entered the U.S. Senate in 1893, serving there for 31 years. As chairman of the Committee on Foreign Relations, he led the successful attack on the Treaty of Versailles and League of Nations after World War I. His position of dominance in Washington extended to its social life. "Nannie" and "Pinkie" (his wife's nickname for the formidable senator) were at the center of the capital's Republican circle. Lodge was at once an intense nationalist and an anglophile, envisioning for America a British imperial destiny. Mr. Dooley lampooned "Hinnery Cabin Lodge's" admiration for all things English and described him as approaching the Court of St. James on hands and knees. Lodge's friendship with Theodore Roosevelt, recorded in one of the most famous correspondences in American politics, began in 1884, when both were new in politics, and survived the younger man's rise to the presidency and even the apostasy (to a Republican regular like Lodge) of his third-party Progressive candidacy in 1912. Henry Adams compared the two friends: "Roosevelts are born and can never be taught," but Lodge was a "creature of teaching . . . at home and happy among the vices and extravagances of Shakespeare — standing first on the social, then on the political foot . . . sometimes bitter, often genial, always intelligent — Lodge had the singular merit of interesting."

LONG, JOHN DAVIS (1838–1915), governor of Massachusetts, U.S. congressman (Rep.), interested in shipping, and Secretary of the Navy, 1897-1902. He was an able, if undistinguished administrator. Long espoused many reform causes, including prohibition, women's suffrage, the abolition of the death penalty, and world peace. His *Journal* is a standard historical source. Long also wrote poetry and volumes on naval affairs and politics.

LOPEZ, JULIANA, daughter of a wealthy landowning Philippine family. An older brother, Sixto, represented the Filipino nationalists outside the islands. In 1902, an older sister, Clemencia, came to America to plead for her three brothers imprisoned by the American authorities. One of them had been an officer in the insurgent army in Batangas province. President Roosevelt turned down her petition (presented by the Boston attorney Louis Brandeis). During her long visit Clemencia was adopted by Boston anti-imperialists and sometimes spoke at their public meetings. The Lopez family of ten brothers and sisters was extraordinarily close and the voluminous correspondence among them during the period of American military occupation is one of the most interesting exhibits printed in the proceedings of the Senate hearings on the Philippines in 1902.

MacARTHUR, ARTHUR (1845–1912), awarded the Congressional Medal of Honor for bravery during the Civil War, served as "Boy Colonel of the West" on the frontier, promoted in 1898 to major general of volunteers, successor in May, 1900, to Major General Elwell Otis as military governor and commanding general in the Philippines. Where his predecessor popularized the view that the insurrection was the work of "outlaws" and "bandits," MacArthur brought a measure of realism to the conflict, recognizing that the insurgents were supported by the "united and apparently spontaneous action of several millions of people." His leadership was not satisfactory to the Administration. William Howard Taft complained to Secretary of War Root in 1900 that "overcaution and timidity led him to adopt a drifting course" because he is "afraid of a congressional investigation." MacArthur was replaced in 1901 when his job was divided into civil and military functions. Taft was made governor general, while the determined Chaffee became commanding general. MacArthur's son

Douglas came honestly by the wisdom: "Anyone who commits the American army on the mainland of Asia ought to have his head examined."

McKINLEY, WILLIAM (1843–1901), twenty-fifth President of the United States. The McKinley Tariff Act of 1890 was the culminating work of six congressional terms during which McKinley became the foremost supporter of the protective tariff. Losing his seat in the 1890 Democratic landslide, he became (with the aggressive help of Cleveland industrialist Mark Hanna) a two-term Ohio governor, and in 1896, the Republican presidential nominee. The bitter election contest with free silver Democrat William Jennings Bryan rewarded McKinley with the first popular majority in a presidential election since 1872. McKinley has had a lackluster reputation among scholars, who tended to agree with the assessment of a contemporary, Charles Francis Adams, that he was a "political invertebrate"; an "Ohio man — no leader, no thinker, no convictions." He is currently enjoying a historical reappraisal. The new view depicts McKinley as an effective, behind-the-scenes political manager, expert in his dealings with Congress, the architect of Republican and national unity at the turn of the century. In his lifetime McKinley's devotion to his invalid wife, solemn dignity, and "ecclesiastical face of the XVth century" inspired an almost awestruck popularity. (He was "the most tender-hearted man I ever met in politics," said New York's "Boss" Platt.) There was an outpouring of public grief when, ten months after his impressive second victory over Bryan, he was assassinated in Buffalo by a Polish immigrant anarchist.

MASON, WILLIAM ERNEST (1850–1921), two-term Republican congressman from Illinois, elected senator in 1897. Mason's reputation as a humorist and storyteller followed him to the Senate, where he became one of the most popular speakers. He fought a losing battle for racial justice, and was a strong supporter of labor rights, attacking trusts and concentrations of capital. Mason was one of the first senators to advocate intervention in Cuba on behalf of the struggling rebels. His opposition to the Philippine War, in defiance of party policy, led the Administration to oppose his reelection, and Mason retired after a single Senate term. Returning to Washington as a congressman-at-large for Illinois in 1917, Mason opposed American entry into World War I and the selective draft. Despite this unpopular stand, he was twice reelected. After the war, he became an active champion of recognition of the Irish Republic.

MYRICK, HERBERT (1860–1927), agricultural publisher, editor, writer, and lobbyist. President of the Phelps Publishing Company of Springfield, Massachusetts, Myrick published and edited many periodicals for farmers. From 1900 to 1911 he published *Good Housekeeping*, developing it into a leading women's magazine, and founded the Good Housekeeping Institute. Myrick promoted many progressive ideas in farming, such as cooperative buying and selling, and the establishment of associations to protect farmers' interests. His Farmers' Political League became a powerful agricultural lobbying group. Myrick saw in American colonial expansion a grave threat to domestic agriculture. As a vice-president of the Anti-Imperialist League, he organized an energetic nationwide campaign to mobilize farmers against the treaty with Spain.

OTIS, ELWELL STEPHEN (1838–1909), army major general, wounded in the Civil War, veteran of Little Big Horn, author of *The Indian Question*. In August, 1898, Otis was made military governor of the Philippines, in command of all civil and military functions. He was known as "the old grandmother" by his subordinates. His tedious attention to detail and inability to delegate responsibility infuriated the military command in Manila. During his entire Philippine service, Otis never visited the field positions of the American forces. His rigid and highly political censorship of press reports provoked correspondents to cable home an unprecedented joint dispatch denying that the "situation was well in hand." The President nonetheless stuck by Otis until he voluntarily resigned his command in 1900. Returning to the U.S. that spring, Otis confidently announced (more than two years before the official termination of the war) that "the thing is entirely over."

PETTIGREW, RICHARD FRANKLIN (1848–1926), first senator from South Dakota, elected in 1889, reelected in 1895 as a Republican, but always at war with the Republican party. He led the Senate fight against the acquisition of Hawaii, then opposed Philippine annexation. Pettigrew battled against private concentrations of economic power and advocated government ownership of railroads and public utilities. He was defeated for reelection to the Senate in 1900, Republican party chairman Hanna personally entering the campaign against him. Pettigrew later charged that money from the interests he attacked found its way to South Dakota to buy his defeat. He vigorously opposed America's entry into World War I. In 1917 he was indicted, but not tried, for publicly stating that the war was waged more for profiteers than for democracy.

PLATT, THOMAS COLLIER (1833–1910), New York Republican politician, and U.S. senator from 1897 to 1909. Allied with Wall Street and the corporations, Platt was the absolute boss of New York State's Republican party in the closing years of the century. He presided over weekly Sunday gatherings at the Fifth Avenue Hotel in Manhattan. There, state political leaders attended "Sunday school" to learn Republican gospel according to Platt. When Governor Theodore Roosevelt refused to respect decisions emanating from Platt's Sunday "Amen Corner," Platt kicked Roosevelt upstairs into the vice-presidential nomination. So certain was he of Roosevelt's prospective political demise in this job that he went to the inauguration joking that he was going to see his old enemy "take the veil." The decline of Platt's power coincided with Roosevelt's elevation to the presidency.

PROCTOR, REDFIELD (1831–1908), Vermont Republican, governor, Secretary of War under Benjamin Harrison, senator from 1891 to his death, interested in agriculture and military affairs. Proctor's intervention helped secure fellow Vermonter George Dewey the command of the Asiatic Squadron. His March, 1898, speech on Spanish brutalities in Cuba was the most influential public utterance of his career. Proctor, known as the "Marble King" for his promotion of his state's major industry, had been president of the Vermont Marble Company, the world's largest marble producer. Years later Elihu Root remarked of this consistent supporter of Republican administrations, "The only trouble with Proctor was that he wanted everything built of Vermont marble."

QUAY, MATTHEW STANLEY (1833–1904), Republican politician, elected U.S. senator from Pennsylvania in 1887 and 1893. In 1899, the Pennsylvania legislature was deadlocked over the reelection of Quay, who had just been indicted for misappropriating state funds. The Pennsylvania governor appointed Quay to fill the vacancy resulting from the legislature's failure to act. The Senate refused to seat him, however. (As an act of revenge against Hanna, who cast the deciding negative vote, Quay joined Platt to force the vice-presidential nomination of Roosevelt, whom Hanna opposed.) In 1901 the Pennsylvania legislature obediently returned Quay to the Senate for a third term. Quay controlled the Republican machine in Pennsylvania for two decades through graft and other forms of political racketeering. His political cunning was thought by some to surpass even that of the masterly Platt of New York.

ROOSEVELT, THEODORE (1858–1919), twenty-sixth President of the United States. Roosevelt was born to a patrician family prominent in New York affairs. The frail and asthmatic boy worked persistently to develop physical strength. After a Harvard education he went West to become a hunter and ranchman. He entered the New York State Assembly in 1881. In only twenty years, he became President of the United States. Along his trajectory were appointments as U.S. Civil Service Commissioner, New York City Police Commissioner, and Assistant Secretary of the Navy. The governorship of New York and the vice-presidency followed. At 42, he was the youngest man ever to serve as President. His two terms in office were marked by a vigorous, highly personal foreign policy, and his never quite realized war against the trusts and "malefactors of great wealth." He received the Nobel Peace Prize in 1906 (the only President awarded this honor) for his mediation of the Russo-Japanese War. Aligning himself with the progressive wing of his party, Roosevelt broke with the Republicans in 1912, and ran unsuccessfully for President as the Bull Moose candidate. Roosevelt advocated the "strenuous life," for nations as well as individuals. His own energy and interests were inexhaustible. In and out of office, he pursued a phenomenally productive and varied career as historian, essayist, naturalist, and outdoorsman. He wrote altogether more than twenty books, in addition to public papers and speeches. His accounts of his own activities were sometimes misleading. Reviewing his book *The Rough Riders*, Mr. Dooley commented on "Tiddy's" none too modest narrative, "If I was him I'd call th' book 'Alone in Cubia.'"

ROOT, ELIHU (1845–1937), important New York corporation lawyer, Secretary of War under McKinley and Roosevelt, later Roosevelt's Secretary of State, elected to the U.S. Senate (Rep. N.Y.) in 1909. As Secretary of War, Root was responsible for prosecuting the Philippine War to its conclusion, and was the chief architect of colonial policy in the Philippines, Cuba, and Puerto Rico. He was a close adviser to McKinley and to Roosevelt, who thought him "the ablest statesman of any country in any time." Roosevelt wanted to make Root his successor ("I would walk on my hands and knees from the White House to the Capitol to see Root made President") but feared opposition to Root's corporate connections. Trained in mathematics by his mathematician father, Root was known for his analytical mind, a "perfect piece of machinery" according to a contemporary. His administrative skills in the reorganization of the War Department earned him the title "father of the modern American army." He was awarded the Nobel Peace Prize in 1912 for his work as Secretary of State in behalf of international arbitration and world peace.

SCHURZ, CARL (1829–1906), minister to Spain under Lincoln, brigadier general in the Union Army, then U.S. senator from Missouri, Secretary of the Interior, journalist, editor (*The Nation* and the New York *Evening Post*), and political reformer. Schurz began his career as a democratic revolutionary. He was forced to flee his native Prussia after the abortive revolution of 1848. In America, he became active in the anti-slavery movement and rose to political prominence as an early champion of the Republican party. Schurz led the liberal revolt against the regular Republican leadership in 1872, later becoming a central figure in the Mugwump reform movement. For many years he was president of the National Civil Service Reform League and the Civil Service Reform Association of New York. Schurz was a persistent critic of foreign expansion. He opposed Grant's scheme to annex Santo Domingo, as well as Hawaiian and Philippine annexation three decades later. Like the foreign-born Carnegie, his opposition to imperialism sprang from a passionate respect for American founding principles. He continued to be a major leader of the Anti-Imperialist League until his death.

SHAFTER, WILLIAM RUFUS (1835–1906), Civil War veteran awarded the Medal of Honor, Indian fighter, advanced to major general of volunteers at the start of the Spanish-American War. Shafter led the expeditionary force to Santiago, Cuba, but owing to tropical illness and his obesity he sat out much of the campaign. He retired from active service in 1899.

SMITH, JACOB HURD (1840–1918), Civil War veteran who later served in the Indian frontier wars, Spanish-American War, and Philippine War, called "Hell-Roaring Jake" for his use of violent language. While in the Philippines he was appointed brigadier general of the U.S. Army. After the massacre at Balangiga in 1901 he was sent to pacify the island of Samar. His instructions to make the countryside a "howling wilderness" and to "kill everyone over ten" led to his court-martial and his forced retirement from active service.

SPOONER, JOHN COIT (1843–1919), prominent corporation lawyer, and three-term U.S. senator from Wisconsin, first elected in 1885. Spooner was floor leader and constitutional adviser of the Senate's ruling Republican hierarchy. For his legal ability he was considered the "most brilliant" and "ablest man" in the Senate. He was the author of countless "Spooner" amendments and compromises, one of which was the 1901 amendment providing for civil government in the Philippines. The last years of his congressional career were marked by a feud with Wisconsin's Progressive leader and junior senator, Robert La Follette.

STOREY, MOORFIELD (1845–1929), well-known Boston lawyer and reformer, briefly president of the American Bar Association, first president of the National Association for the Advancement of Colored People. Storey began his public career as secretary to the Massachusetts abolitionist senator, Charles Sumner. He participated in the Mugwump reform movement, becoming chairman of the Massachusetts Reform Club. He ran unsuccessfully for Congress in 1900 as an antiwar candidate, and was frequently mentioned as the anti-imperialists' presidential choice in the event of a third-party campaign. Storey's ardent championship of the Filipino right to self-government led to his deepening involvement in the race problem at home. In public addresses he consistently stressed the connection between imperialism and racism: "The worst result of imperialism . . . is the race problem at our own doors . . . Our crime in Asia will be punished on our own soil." Storey succeeded George Boutwell as president of the New England Anti-Imperialist League in 1905, and for the next quarter-century led its dwindling forces in the fight for Philippine independence. Five years later he became the first president of the N.A.A.C.P., serving until his death.

TAFT, WILLIAM HOWARD (1857–1930), twenty-seventh President of the United States. McKinley chose this genial, obese Ohio federal judge to become president of the second Philippine Commission, and later the first civil governor of the Philippine Islands. As colonial administrator, Taft worked hard to attract American capital to the islands, and to develop Philippine markets for American goods. His attitude toward the natives, or "little brown brothers" as he called them, was often sympathetic (though always paternalistic), and he was a generally popular governor. Twice he refused an appointment to the U.S. Supreme Court, a post he coveted, in order to continue his colonizing work. Taft became Roosevelt's Secretary of War in 1904, and his hand-picked successor four years later when the President declined to run for a third term. During his administration, the active intervention of the federal government to protect American investments abroad, or "dollar diplomacy," became a well-defined policy. But Taft lacked skill as a political leader. ("Politics makes me sick," he confided to friends.) His leadership was compromised by the growing insurgency of Republican progressives in the Senate, and after 1910 by a break with Roosevelt, who dismissed him as a "good lieutenant but a poor captain." In a three-way presidential contest in 1912, Roosevelt, candidate of the Progressive (Bull Moose) Party, split the Republican vote with Taft, sending Woodrow Wilson to the White House. When at last President Harding appointed "Big Bill" U.S. Chief Justice in 1921, Taft realized his lifetime ambition. He is the only man to have held both the nation's highest executive and judicial posts.

TILLMAN, BENJAMIN RYAN (1847–1918), governor of South Carolina and four-term U.S. senator. An Edgefield County farmer who led a vigilante group during Reconstruction, Tillman developed a statewide reputation with rousing speeches demanding agrarian reform. He was twice elected governor as the farmers' candidate. His two terms in office displayed a now familiar southern combination of militant white supremacy and radical agrarianism. Under his leadership South Carolina became the second state to disfranchise the Negro. He won election to the Senate in 1894 in a colorful campaign that attacked President Cleveland's conservatism: "I'll stick my pitchfork into his old ribs." In the Senate "Pitchfork Ben" Tillman became the outstanding defender of southern lynch law and Negro disfranchisement. Republicans frequently left the chamber when he spoke. Belligerent and occasionally violent, the one-eyed Tillman (his left eye was lost after a Civil War illness) "never bored anyone," as Lodge remarked. In 1902, he started a fist fight with the junior South Carolina senator, McLaurin, on the Senate floor, in a dispute over McLaurin's vote to ratify the treaty with Spain three years earlier. The incident caused President Roosevelt to withdraw a White House dinner invitation to Tillman. Curiously, a *New York Times* Washington correspondent characterized Tillman's relations with the black race as loving and tender — "There is not a Negro who has ever met him whose face will not light up if you mention Tillman's name."

TWAIN, MARK, pen name of Samuel Langhorne Clemens (1835–1910). Twain was one of many literary figures and journalists (among them William Dean Howells, Edgar Lee Masters, Edward Arlington Robinson, and E. L. Godkin) associated with anti-imperialism. He became a vehement critic of the Philippine War upon his return to America in late 1900 after a long exile abroad. "To the Person Sitting in Darkness," his savage satire of missionary imperialism, created a sensation when it was published in the February, 1901, *North American Review*, and was widely reprinted as an Anti-Imperialist League pamphlet. His ironic "Defence of General Funston," published the following year, attacked Funston's use of bribery and pretense to capture Aguinaldo. (The article was prompted by Funston's denunciation of anti-imperialists as "traitors." Twain responded

that he would "rather be a traitor than an archangel" if it were trea-
son to demand that the U.S. free the Philippines.) "Comments on
the Killing of Six Hundred Moros," a masterpiece of Twainian invec-
tive, was written after the slaughter of Moro civilians by American
soldiers in 1906, and published posthumously.

WHEELER, JOSEPH (1836–1906), soldier and U.S. congressman
(1881–1900) from Alabama. His remarkable career in the Confederate Army made "Fighting Joe" a figure of great popularity throughout the South. After the outbreak of the Spanish-American War,
President McKinley called him from Congress (where he was ranking
Democrat on the Ways and Means Committee) to serve as second
in command of the American forces in Cuba. His appointment was
seen as an attempt to further heal sectional animosities. "Fighting
Joe's" willingness to risk his men's lives in rash attacks against the
enemy finally led General Shafter to order him to "attempt no more
battles." After the war with Spain he was sent to the Philippines as
brigadier general of volunteers. General MacArthur resisted his im-
petuous attempts to engage the Filipinos after the outbreak of hostilities and relegated him to a minor role in the campaign.

CHRONOLOGY

1895

February 24   Insurrection against Spain breaks out in Cuba.

1896

February 10   Spanish Governor General ("Butcher") Weyler arrives in Cuba and begins ruthless suppression of revolt. Hundreds of thousands reconcentrated from countryside into garrison towns; many die of starvation and disease. Repressive measures arouse sympathy in U.S.

August 26   Filipinos initiate insurrection against Spain.

November 3   William McKinley wins decisive victory over free silver candidate William Jennings Bryan in watershed presidential election. Republicans control Congress.

1897

March 4   McKinley inaugurated as twenty-fifth President of the United States.

April 19   Theodore Roosevelt takes office as Assistant Secretary of the Navy.

December 14   Treaty of Biak-na-Bato ends Filipino rebellion; leaders, including Emilio Aguinaldo, exiled to Hong Kong.

1898

January 3 Commodore George Dewey assumes command of the Asiatic Squadron.

January 25 U.S.S. *Maine* arrives at Havana on "friendly visit."

February 15 *Maine* blown up and sunk in Havana Harbor — two hundred sixty American sailors killed in mysterious explosion.

February 25 Acting Secretary of the Navy Roosevelt orders Pacific fleet, under Commodore Dewey, to Philippines, with instructions to engage the Spanish fleet there in case of war.

March 17 Senator Proctor of Vermont, not generally regarded as a jingo, delivers powerful speech to Senate on sufferings of reconcentrados. Entire nation is aroused.

March 28 Naval court of inquiry reports to Congress that *Maine* was destroyed by explosion of a submarine mine, but does not fix responsibility for the incident. Nevertheless, public blames Spain.

April 9 In response to U.S. demands, Spain agrees to suspend hostilities.

April 11 McKinley sends message to Congress asking for the "forceful intervention" of the U.S. to establish peace in Cuba.

April 19 Congress adopts joint resolution recognizing Cuban independence and authorizing the President to use military force to secure Spain's withdrawal from the island. In a final clause (the Teller Amendment) Congress disclaims intention of exercising sovereignty over Cuba.

April 25 U.S. formally declares war against Spain, made retroactive to April 21.

May 1 U.S. Pacific fleet under Dewey destroys Spanish fleet at Manila Bay in spectacular battle — Spanish losses, three hundred eighty-one killed and wounded; American casualties, eight wounded.

May 6 — Roosevelt resigns navy post to become lieutenant colonel of First United States Volunteer Cavalry (the "Rough Riders").

May 19 — At U.S. request, Aguinaldo returns to Philippines, organizes large native army to help fight Spain. American officials indicate U.S. will support Philippine independence, although no agreement is signed.

June 12 — Aguinaldo issues Philippine Declaration of Independence.

June 14 — Army under General William Shafter leaves for Cuba.

June 15 — First anti-imperialist protest held at Faneuil Hall, Boston.

June 20 — Spanish governor on Pacific island of Guam surrenders to commander of U.S.S. *Charleston*.

June 22 — U.S. expeditionary force debarks near Santiago. American troops defeat Spanish forces at Las Guasimas in first land battle of war.

June 23 — Filipinos organize "revolutionary government" under Aguinaldo, whose forces hold all Luzon, largest Philippine island, excluding city of Manila.

June 30 — U.S. expeditionary force arrives at Manila.

July 1 — U.S. forces defeat Spanish at battles of El Caney and San Juan Hill at cost of 1,572 casualties. Roosevelt, leading unmounted Rough Riders in daring charge up Kettle Hill, becomes a national hero.

July 3 — U.S. Navy destroys Spanish fleet in battle of Santiago.

July 7 — McKinley signs resolution annexing Hawaii to the U.S. (Annexation, repeatedly blocked by former

President Cleveland and Senate, gained new support during war.)

July 17 Cuban campaigns end with surrender of Spanish garrison at Santiago.

July 25 U.S. force under Major General Nelson A. Miles lands at Guanica, Puerto Rico. His well-planned campaign there meets only token enemy resistance.

August 12 U.S. and Spain sign protocol ending hostilities.

August 13 U.S. forces with aid of Philippine rebels attack Manila, unaware of armistice. After nominal defense, Spaniards surrender city.

August 28 Major General Elwell Otis assumes command of U.S. forces in Philippines.

October 1 Treaty negotiations between U.S. and Spain open in Paris.

November 8 Theodore Roosevelt elected governor of New York.

November 19 New England Anti-Imperialist League established to oppose acquisition of Philippine Islands — officers include George Boutwell, Andrew Carnegie, Samuel Gompers, Charles Francis Adams, Grover Cleveland.

December 10 Treaty ending Spanish-American War signed in Paris; Spain frees Cuba, cedes Puerto Rico and Guam, and sells the Philippines to U.S. for twenty million dollars. Treaty marks end of Spanish rule in Western Hemisphere.

December 21 McKinley issues proclamation declaring U.S. policy of "benevolent assimilation" in Philippines. Warns natives against resistance to U.S. rule.

1899

January 4 McKinley submits Treaty of Paris to U.S. Senate for confirmation.

January 7	Filipinos resolve to fight for independence if U.S. insists on annexation.
January 23	Philippine Repubic inaugurated. Constitution provides for a "popular, representative, and responsible" government.
February 4	Hostilities in Philippines commence when American patrol near Manila fires on Filipino soldier. General firing erupts, and MacArthur, the American commander on scene, orders troops to advance.
February 6	By one vote beyond required two-thirds majority, Senate affirms treaty with Spain.
February 14	Bacon Amendment, disclaiming intention to exercise permanent control over Philippines, defeated by tie-breaking vote of Vice-President Hobart.
March 31	U.S. forces under General MacArthur capture insurgent capital of Malolos, but find city burned and deserted.
April 28	Philippine emissaries request armistice, Otis demands unconditional surrender.
July 9	War correspondents in Philippines jointly protest official "ultra-optimistic" battle reports.
October 17–18	National anti-imperialist convention at Chicago. American Anti-Imperialist League established with George Boutwell as president.
November 19	U.S. forces capture last insurgent capital at Bayambang. Filipino Congress disbanded; Aguinaldo flees to mountains. American officials claim formal rebellion ends with collapse of Philippine Republic and dispersion of Aguinaldo's army, assert that guerrillas in field are now merely "bandits."
November 21	Death of Vice-President Garrett Hobart.

1900

January 6   Anti-imperialists meet at Plaza Hotel, New York City, to discuss formation of third party.

May 5   Major General Arthur MacArthur replaces Otis as Commanding General in Philippines.

June 3   Philippine Commission, headed by William Howard Taft, arrives in Manila.

June 19–21   Republican National Convention at Philadelphia nominates McKinley and Bryan. McKinley will conduct a front porch campaign, never leaving home, while Roosevelt campaigns vigorously. "Prosperity," "Bryanism," and a defense of the President's Philippine policy are major themes.

July 4–6   Democratic National Convention at Kansas City nominates William Jennings Bryan and Adlai E. Stevenson of Illinois. Imperialism is the "paramount issue."

August 15–16   At Liberty Congress in Indianapolis, anti-imperialists reject third-party campaign, endorse Bryan "as the most effective means of crushing imperialism." Repudiating Democratic party's racist policies in the South, they assert that Declaration of Independence should apply to "the Negro race in America as well as the Filipinos."

August 31   Commanding General MacArthur cables that there is little improvement in military situation, with the insurgents holding out until after election.

November 6   McKinley reelected by large popular plurality, though many voters stay home. Republicans retain control of House and Senate.

December 20   MacArthur orders more stringent policy against insurgents.

1901

March 2   As rider to army appropriation bill, Congress adopts Platt Amendment, establishing a quasi-protectorate over Cuba; also Spooner Amendment, facilitating transfer of power in Philippines from military to civil authorities.

March 4   McKinley inaugurated for second term as President; Roosevelt sworn in as Vice-President.

March 23   Colonel Frederick Funston, using native scouts disguised as insurgents, captures Aguinaldo in mountain hideout. Rebellion continues under leadership of Generals Malvar, Lukban, and others.

May 27   Supreme Court, in series of decisions known as the "Insular Cases," rejects principle popularly known as "the Constitution follows the flag." Court rules that although territories annexed after Spanish-American War are not foreign nations, constitutional rights of U.S. citizens do not automatically apply to their inhabitants, who are to be subject to special laws of Congress.

July 1   William Howard Taft becomes first civil governor of Philippines. Major General Adna Chaffee replaces MacArthur as commanding general.

September 6   Polish anarchist Leon Czolgosz shoots President McKinley at Pan-American Exposition, Buffalo, New York. President dies the following week.

September 14   Theodore Roosevelt takes oath of office at Buffalo as twenty-sixth President of the United States.

September 28   Natives working on army outpost in the seemingly friendly town of Balangiga, on the island of Samar, attack unarmed, breakfasting troops. Forty-eight U.S. soldiers brutally slaughtered in worst enemy surprise attack of war.

October	Brigadier General "Hell-Roaring Jake" Smith orders that Samar be made a "howling wilderness."
December	Brigadier General James Bell adopts drastic measures in Batangas province, including reconcentration of civilians.

1902

January 13	Senator Hoar presents anti-imperialist resolution asking congressional investigation of Philippine atrocities.
January 31	Senate Committee on Philippines, chaired by Henry Cabot Lodge, opens hearings.
March 21	Trial of Major Waller and Lieutenant Day for murder of native guides on island of Samar begins at Manila. Defense pleads not guilty on grounds that Waller was following orders of General Smith.
April 14	Soldiers begin testimony to Senate Philippine Committee on army's regular use of water torture and other cruelties against natives.
April 15	President Roosevelt orders court-martial of General Smith and "sweeping" investigation of atrocities.
April 16	Aguinaldo's successor, Malvar, surrenders to U.S. authorities, last Filipino general to yield.
April 28	Anti-imperialists form committee to investigate army conduct in Philippines. Its members (who include Carl Schurz, Moorfield Storey, Herbert Welsh, and Charles Francis Adams) provide information and witnesses to Democratic minority of Senate Committee on Philippines.
June 28	Committee on Philippines adjourns hearings over protest by Democratic minority.

July 1 Congress passes Philippine Government Act, declaring the Philippine Islands an unorganized territory under U.S. supervision.

July 4 President Roosevelt formally terminates the war, thanking army for its work. Islands placed under civil control.

July 14 Roosevelt approves lenient findings of Smith courtmartial, but retires Smith from active army service.

July 22 In open letter to President, anti-imperialist investigating committee rejects Roosevelt's characterization of Smith conduct as "exceptional." Provides further evidence of army atrocities and demands new investigation, which Roosevelt declines to authorize.

September 25 Anti-imperialists publish review of army policy in the Philippines (Storey and Codman's *Marked Severities*), charging Secretary of War Root with responsibility for army cruelties.

1903

March 19 Boston citizens hold open hearings to protest "suppression of truth" about army conduct in Philippines.